THE INTELLIGENT GUIDE TO CASINO GAMING

THE INTELLIGENT GUIDE TO CASINO GAMING

Sylvester Suzuki

Intelligent Games Publishing

Baltimore

The Intelligent Guide to Casino Gaming

Copyright © 2011 by Intelligent Games Publishing
An imprint of Chartley Publishing, LLC

For information contact:
Intelligent Games Publishing
P. O. Box 6705, Baltimore, MD 21285
www.Intelligent-Games.com
service@intelligent-games.com

ISBN-13   978-0-9677551-5-1
Library of Congress Control Number: 2010939359
Ebook edition also available.
Ebook edition ISBN-13: 978-0-9677551-8-2

Book Cover Writing: Graham Van Dixhorn, Write to Your Market, Inc.

Publisher's Cataloging-In-Publication Data
(Prepared by The Donohue Group, Inc.)
Suzuki, Sylvester.
  The intelligent guide to casino gaming / Sylvester Suzuki.

    p. : ill. ; cm.

  Includes bibliographical references and index.
  ISBN-13: 978-0-9677551-5-1
  ISBN-10: 0-9677551-5-8

  1. Gambling. 2. Gambling systems. 3. Game theory. 4. Casinos. I. Title.

GV1301 .S99 2011
795   2010939359

Contents

List of Tables and Figures

Baccarat

Blackjack

Craps

Roulette

Poker-Themed Games

Keno

Slots and Video Poker

Sports Betting

Foreword

Sam Braids

I had my first casino experience a few years after I became old enough to gamble. My wife and I were on a road trip to California and we stopped to visit some friends in Las Vegas. Our friends lived in a residential area, away from the strip, and described living in Vegas as ordinary. With the exception of slot machines in the supermarkets, living in the world-famous gambling Mecca differed little from living in any other large city.

Since we were guests who had never been to Vegas, our friends took us out to experience the strip and see what a casino is about. Surprisingly, I discovered that casinos could be very affordable venues for entertainment. At that time, the mid-1980s, the casinos served all-you-could-eat buffets for less than $10 per person. Our hosts joked that Las Vegas was the only city where eating out was cheaper than cooking your own meals. My wife and I played quarter slot machines and combined, lost about $10 that evening. But, waitresses served free drinks of our choice while we played. Overall the night was a fun double date that cost much less than many alternative forms of entertainment.

Of course my wife and I didn't come expecting to get rich. We had realistic expectations for gaming outcomes, a limited budget, and we didn't bet on games that we didn't understand. The affordable entertainment we experienced was subsidized by gamblers with bigger budgets, many of whom had unrealistic expectations and didn't always understand the games they played. As I left the casino that night, I passed a bank of slot machines that took $100 tokens for each spin, and was mystified by the sight of people actually playing them.

I still enjoy visiting casinos, and I still find it a very affordable form of entertainment. Living on the East coast, I usually visit Atlantic City each summer for the poker games, and as an inexpensive outing to an ocean beach. The casino comps me a room and some of my food based on my poker play, waitresses serve free drinks while I play, and there is still time to relax on the beach and stroll the boardwalk. Depending on how I do at the poker tables, I can often break-even or show a small net gain for the entire outing. Even if my poker results are poor, I am still far ahead compared to a beach outing without casinos, where I have to pay for everything.

Of course I've played lots of poker, and I've dabbled with blackjack. But, until I read Sylvester's book I knew nothing about the details of the other table games. Part of the reason for this ignorance is a credibility problem with many of the other books written on gambling. Most of these books have titles such as: *Winning Casino Craps, Gamble to Win Roulette* and *Powerful Profits From Keno*. Books with the words: winning, win, or profits, in the title lose me before I open them up. On a given day, you might win at craps, roulette, keno, etc. But, you certainly can't make winning a goal because there is no credible way of achieving it. These games are relentlessly negative expectation games that if you play long enough will cost you money. As much as we would like to think of ourselves as special, no one is exempt from the mathematical laws of probabilities.

The fact is casinos make money by offering a wide variety of games in which they have an advantage. In other words, the casinos win at gambling, and it is those winnings that provide all the freebees. However, casino patrons have a bewildering array of choices for placing bets and you might be surprised to learn that the house advantage varies considerably among the bets offered. Some bets have expectations that are close to even money, while others can have a 35% or more advantage for the house.

Often gamblers are enticed to make the worse bets because these bets have the largest payoffs. But, your chances of winning money increase if you restrict yourself to the bets with the smallest house advantage. Because games of chance have high variabilities in outcomes, it is within the realm of possibility to walk out a winner after a short stay. That possibility is more likely if you stick to bets in which the casino's advantage is close to even money. In those cases a fluctuation in your favor is more likely to put you ahead. Chasing big payoffs by making bets in which the house has a large advantage is more likely to send you home a loser.

There are some instances in games such as blackjack and poker, in which a skilled player might have an edge. But usually the edge is small and exploiting it for a meaningful profit would require putting large sums of money at risk repeatedly over an extended period of time. Most people have more productive, less risky uses for their time and money. The dream of becoming rich from a casino visit or making a living gambling is just that for most people—a dream.

However, most people have realistic expectations when they visit a casino. In fact, the vast majority of the millions of people who visit casinos each year go for entertainment and recreation. They do not expect to become rich, and only a few have gambling problems. (If you have a gambling problem you should contact Gamblers Anonymous at http://gamblersanonymous.org and not read this book.) Most casino patrons just want to enjoy themselves and get the most value for their entertainment dollar. This book is written for that vast majority. It shows how get the most out of your casino experience—the most value and the most fun.

Sylvester has written a frank, honest guide, to all the popular casino games. After reading this book you will be able to play these games with confidence, and know which bets to place and which bets to avoid. You will find none of the false promises and unsubstantiated claims found in most books on gaming. Instead you will find a treasure trove of information that will help you budget and plan your casino visits. Take this book with you and use it as a reference. If you adhere to the strategies Sylvester presents you can substantially reduce the casino's edge and still take advantage of all the discounted rooms and meals.

The fact is most of the games offered in a casino are simpler than they appear. Don't be fooled by sellers of complex betting systems with big claims but questionable results. Learning the optimal strategy for each game is not difficult. If you stick to the optimal strategy you will save yourself a great deal of money in the long-run, and increase your chances of coming out ahead in the short-run. You can take advantage of all the freebees casinos offer while giving very little of it back at the tables.

Preface

One afternoon, I was on the freeway en route to a nearby card casino where I had planned to participate in a poker tournament. Since it was still a little early, I decided to stop by at a Barnes and Noble bookstore. As is usually the case when I'm in a bookstore, I wandered over to the Games section.

With the recent explosion of interest in all forms of gambling, the Games section had more than doubled in size since my last visit. Due to the popularity of poker tournaments on television, most of the new books on gambling pertain to poker. However, there has been a spillover effect on all types of books on gaming, even on books that have not been seen on bookshelves for several years.

On the bookshelf were books with such intriguing titles as *Winning at Baccarat*, *Powerful Profits from Keno*, and *How to Win at Roulette*. Win at baccarat, keno, and roulette? These are all negative expectation games in which the casino has a mathematical advantage over the player on every single bet, and there is no way that the player can do anything to offset the house advantage. Therefore, the suggestion that a casino patron can be taught how to win at such games is somewhat akin to suggesting that someone can be taught how to win a state lottery. It is true that in the short run, casino patrons sometimes do win at baccarat, keno, and roulette. However, it is also true that there are winners in the state lottery. In games in which the casino has a mathematical advantage on every bet, the only way that a patron can be taught how to win is to teach him how to manipulate the game, either by rigging the machinery or by corrupting personnel who run the game.

Somewhat different than games such as baccarat, keno, and roulette is blackjack (also known as 21). In blackjack, with a fresh deck of cards, the casino has a slight mathematical advantage over the player. However, depending on the composition of the cards that remain in the unused portion of the deck, the advantage sometimes shifts to the player. For this reason, a player who has the ability to maintain an accurate count of the cards remaining in the deck can reasonably expect to win by betting small amounts when the deck is favorable to the casino and betting larger amounts when the deck is favorable to the player. However, this temporary advantage to the player is usually very small and it requires considerable expertise to determine when conditions are favorable for the player. It also requires patience and guile to wait for such a favorable condition to arise and capitalize on the situation without arousing the suspicion of casino employees who are trained to recognize card counters.

Also different is poker. When playing poker in a casino, the patron is not actually competing against the casino. He is merely paying the casino for the privilege of playing in the casino. In essence, he is like a tenant who is paying rent. All that the casino poker player need do to win is to outplay other players at his table by a sufficient margin to overcome the amount that the casino is charging him for rent. However, due to the generally high skill level of most casino poker players, and the high rent, only a small number of very skillful players are capable of actually making a living by playing poker in the casinos. A somewhat larger number of players are, however, capable of consistently winning smaller amounts.

Slot machines were originally relatively simple mechanical devices that were activated by dropping a coin into a slot and then pulling down on a long steel arm that protruded from the side of the machine. Once activated, these machines, which for good reason became known as "one-armed bandits," automatically continued on to conclusion of play. Because these machines required very little space, were easy to administer and could be readily programmed to generate the desired level of profit, they gradually became the primary source of revenues for gambling casinos.

Although on the surface many modern slot machines closely resemble their earlier ancestors, there is little resemblance on the inside. No longer a simple mechanical device, the modern slot machine is a complex computer controlled-electronic device. From the standpoint of the player, however, these modern slot machines have the same basic drawback. They are programmed to give the casino a consistent mathematical advantage over the player and there is no way for the player to compensate for the house advantage.

An offshoot of these computerized slot machines are game machines that during the course of play give the player an option that can affect the chances of winning. In fact, studies indicate that with perfectly optimal selection on every play, it is possible for the expert player to gain a small fractional advantage over the house on some video poker machines that have a progressive jackpot. However, very few players are capable of attaining the required level of expertise.

In the last few years, billions of dollars have been invested in order to build huge, luxury casinos across the United States. Notwithstanding the impression that one might get from Hollywood, the mainstay of the American casino is not the glamorous James Bond type character that is depicted in the movies, but the average working American. These are the hardworking men and women who generate huge profits for casinos by laying down small bets at the gaming tables and dropping a few days' wages into the slot machines. What are the prospects that one of these small fry will walk away from the casino a winner? In honesty, not very good.

However, the purpose of this book is not to discourage the reader from visiting a casino. The purpose is to give you an honest, objective appraisal in the hope that you can improve your chances of leaving as a winner by taking advantage of the most favorable betting situations that are available and availing yourself of all the complimentary gifts, coupons and discounts that the casino offers. In this way, you will be able to enjoy more, lose less and have a reasonable expectation of sometimes leaving the casino with more money in your pocket than when you entered the casino.

1. Casino Gaming

Until 1988 when Congress passed the Indian Gaming Regulatory Act that legalized Nevada style gaming on Indian land, Atlantic City and the state of Nevada had a virtual monopoly on the extremely lucrative casino gaming industry in the United States. Therefore, to no one's surprise, immediately following passage of the act, Indian casinos sprouted up across the country. The largest of these casinos are now huge, mega-resorts that enjoy revenues exceeding one billion dollars annually. Why is casino gaming so lucrative? Quite simply, because of the house advantage.

The House Advantage

On table games, the casino insures that it will have a house advantage by paying out less than the true odds. For example, in roulette, there are 38 slots in the rotating wheel. Therefore, the true odds of selecting the correct number is one in thirty-eight, which is usually expressed as odds of 37 to 1. If true odds were paid, since the winning bettor should be entitled to return of the original dollar that he had bet, he should be paid $38. However, the casino returns only $36 to the winning bettor, which means that the casino will pay off at odds of 35 to 1. The difference of $2 means that the casino is enjoying a house advantage of 5.26% (2/38 = 5.26%) on each single number bet that is made at a roulette table.

On slot machines and video gaming machines, the casino insures that it will have a house advantage by programming machines to pay out less than it takes in. In general, these machines are programmed to pay out from a low of 85% to a high of 98%. However, in a few instances, when a progressive jackpot increases to a very high level, the actual payout rate on a machine may temporarily increase to over 100%. This does not mean, however, that the casino is losing money on such machines because players who had previously played the machine generated the money that will be needed to pay the jackpot. Trust me on this one. Casinos are in business to make a profit and in the long run, with the possible exception of a machine that pays off on a large, multiple-machine jackpot, each machine and table will take in more money than it will pay out. By this, I do not mean to imply that they will win enough to pay all related expenses, because expenses, especially personnel expenses at a table, may be high. However, in the long-run, each machine and table will take in more money than it will pay out. With an unrelenting house advantage, that is a mathematical certainty.

Except in a few unique circumstances that are explained in subsequent chapters of this book, the house will enjoy at least a slight house advantage at every venue in the casino. In order to have a realistic chance of sometimes leaving the casino a winner, it is imperative that you learn how to minimize the house advantage. This I hope to help you do by pointing out in the following chapters the most favorable games and betting situations.

Betting Systems

Over the years, countless betting systems have been developed in order to help the average Joe or Jane beat the house. The most famous of these systems is the Martingale system which is based on the self-evident knowledge that if a player makes the same even money (or close to even money) bet over and over, he is certain to eventually win at least once. Therefore, according to proponents of this system, all the player need do in order to enjoy a small but steady income is to keep doubling his bet until he wins, then go back to making his starting small bet. This means that if the player's basic bet is $10, he will bet $10 on his first hand. If he loses that bet, he will bet $20 on his next hand. If he loses on his second hand, he will make a $40 bet on his third hand, etc. The cumulative result of using this system, assuming that the player has lost each of his previous bets, is summarized below.

Martingale Betting System

	Amount Bet	Cumulative Amount Bet
1st Bet	$10	$10
2nd Bet	$20	$30
3rd Bet	$40	$70
4th Bet	$80	$150
5th Bet	$160	$310
6th Bet	$320	$630
7th Bet	$640	$1270
8th Bet	$1280	$2550
9th Bet	$2560	$5110

As mentioned earlier, casinos are not in business to gamble. They are in business to make a profit. Therefore, in order to protect themselves from possibly heavy losses in the event that a high roller should win some huge bets, casinos have limits on the amount that may be bet in the casino. This betting limit is also looked upon with favor by casino management because it would tend to discourage thoughts of possible collusion between players and employees. Usually, the maximum bet allowed at a table will be approximately 100 times the minimum bet allowed at the table. This means that if a player has a run of bad luck, the Martingale system cannot protect him from suffering huge losses, even if the player has a virtually unlimited bankroll.

Probably the simplest betting system is usually referred to as the compounded betting system. With this system, if a player wins a bet, he will compound his bet a predetermined number of times. The cumulative result of using this system, assuming that the player has won each preceding bet, is shown next.

Compounded Betting System

	Amount Bet	Cumulative Amount Won
1st Bet	$10	$10
2nd Bet	$20	$30
3rd Bet	$40	$70
4th Bet	$80	$150
5th Bet	$160	$310
6th Bet	$320	$630
7th Bet	$640	$1270
8th Bet	$1280	$2550
9th Bet	$2560	$5110

Notice that the numbers in this table are identical to the numbers in the previous table for the Martingale system. It is the third column heading that changes from "cumulative amount bet" to "cumulative amount won." That means the compounded betting system is basically the philosophical opposite of the Martingale system. For the compounded system the player is parlaying house money until he loses, in contrast to the Martingale system in which he increases his own contributions until he wins. Since it is obvious that the house will eventually win a hand, few practitioners of this system will proceed beyond the third bet. However, by then, the basic $10 bettor will have won $70. In addition to making it possible to cash in on a hot streak, this system has the advantage of eliminating the possibility of losing a catastrophic amount on any single hand.

New betting systems are continuously being developed. Some systems that "guarantee" profits are even being offered for sale on the Internet. Save your money! Every betting system that has ever been developed, including the two that were discussed above, has one fatal, common weakness. They do nothing to help overcome the house advantage. Therefore, in the long run, they cannot possibly help you win money in the casinos.*

*The house advantage arises because each bet the player places has a negative "expected value." In *The Two Headed Quarter: How to See Through Deceptive Numbers and Save Money on Everything You Buy,* (Baltimore, MD: Chartley Publishing, 2007), Joseph Ganem explains that "the expected value of a bet is independent of its size." That means "there exists no system for varying bet sizes that can profit over the long run if the expected values of the bets are negative."

Limit on Payouts

Almost all casinos have limits on the amount that will be paid for any winning bet hand. For example, some keno lounges limit the maximum individual payout to $100,000. As a result, a $10 ticket on which all 15 numbers that were selected appear on the keno board might be worth no more than a $1 ticket upon which the same numbers had been selected.

In other cases, a limit is applied to the combined total of all winning tickets during a specific drawing. If such had been the case in the example mentioned in the previous paragraph, payment for either winning ticket might well have been even less than $100,000.

In a casino, there is no greater frustration than being told that the lifestyle-changing jackpot you thought you had just hit may not be as earth-shattering as you had thought. When playing keno or any other game, such as Let It Ride, in which a relatively small wager might result in a potentially huge payout, always inquire about a possible limit on the amount that will be paid. Although it is highly unlikely that you will ever hit on such a long-shot bet, in order to avoid the possibility of getting a rude shock, check this out and consider sizing your bets accordingly.

Budgeting for a Casino Visit

Your visit to a casino, whether it is a one-day visit or an extended vacation should be a fun experience. It is no fun dodging bill collectors or worrying about how you are going to make your next mortgage payment. Therefore, it is extremely important to know how to plan wisely when preparing to visit a casino.

From a budgeting perspective, the only difference between a trip to the casino and any other recreational facility is that a casino trip requires that allowance be made for possible gambling losses. Because of the unpredictable nature of gambling, it is extremely difficult to budget for gambling losses. A $100 stake for a recreational slot machine player might be adequate for a whole day. However, it could also be gone in only a few minutes.

There is even the possibility that you might be ahead at the end of the day.

Before visiting a casino, always establish an upper limit on the amount of money that you will allow yourself to lose. For a one-day visit, a reasonable upper limit might be the amount of excess cash that you took with you to the casino. If you lose the amount that you have established as your upper limit, be resolved that you will quit and go home. **Make no charges to your credit card.** Don't try to borrow a few bucks from a friend. Just go home and sleep it off.

Many vacation trips have been cut short because the entire amount that was budgeted for a vacation was lost prematurely at one of the gaming tables. If you are on a multiple-day trip, establish a firm upper limit on the amount that you will allow yourself to lose each day. If you lose that amount, take a break. Go for a swim, see a show, or go for a long walk. Among inexperienced, and even some experienced gamblers, there is a tendency to try to quickly recoup losses by increasing the size of bets. In casino parlance, this is known as "chasing losses." Never chase losses in this manner. That is a virtual blueprint for disaster. If you must gamble a little more, at least have the good sense to wind down by stepping down to a lower level. However, it probably would have been wiser to start more conservatively at a lower level to begin the day. That will help avoid catastrophic losses and give you the chance to end the day on a high note with some big winning bets that you might be able to afford.

Casino Comps

In the vernacular of the casino gambler, "comp" is an abbreviation for complimentary. Since the dictionary defines "complimentary" as something that is given free of charge, most casino comps are not really complimentary. They are something that has been earned by patronizing the casino. In a few cases, a comp is given after-the-fact as when a room rate is reduced at check-out time because a customer has wagered a specific amount at a slot machine or a gaming table. There are, however, a few truly free comps in casinos.

One of the truly free comps in casinos is the free drink. If you are presentably dressed and even look like you might be engaging in some form of gaming, in many casinos you can get a free drink simply by flagging down one of the cocktail waitresses that are constantly circulating around throughout the casino. Many casinos even have free non-alcoholic beverage stands where people can help themselves to a free soft drink or cup of coffee. No limit, no charge and no questions asked.

Among the best of the free comps, especially for senior citizens, are the free charter buses that many casinos provide to large metropolitan areas. In some cases, this service is provided only on weekdays. However, in many cases, the service is provided seven days a week. In conducting research for this book, the author visited several Indian casinos that provide such service to metropolitan Los Angeles. In addition to the free transportation, upon arrival at the casino, passengers are given a small voucher that can be put into a slot machine or exchanged for cash at a cashier's cage. At one of the casinos, on a designated day of the week, senior citizens are given a significant discount at one of the casino restaurants. At another casino, a free slot tournament is conducted for senior citizens one day a week and small prizes, as well as free buffet tickets, are awarded to the winners of each session of the tournament. If interested in getting similar freebies, if you live within relatively easy commuting distance from a casino, especially an Indian casino, give the casino a call. You might be surprised to learn about what is available in your area.

Not surprisingly, because slot machines generate the overwhelming bulk of revenues for the typical casino, points earned by playing these machines account for most of the points that are earned by casino patrons. Virtually every casino now has what is commonly referred to as a slot club. It is very easy to join. All you need do is show a photo ID card and almost instantly, you will be issued a plastic membership card. When the card is inserted into a slot machine, a record will be made of your bets and points will be credited to your account based on the size of your bets and the number of bets that were made. Points are also awarded for play at gaming tables. However, at a gaming table, it is usually necessary to give your card to the dealer or pit boss* and ask that you be rated for assignment of possible points. Another reason for joining the slot club is that merely by getting on the membership roster, you could start receiving useful information and/or valuable coupons in the mail. Since membership is free, it is recommended that you always join the slot club before playing in a casino.

Most casinos issue comp points based on the amount that the casino expects to earn from your play. For this reason, comps for high rollers are usually much more generous than they are for low rollers. However, with a sound knowledge of how the comp system, with its many coupons and freebies actually works, even low rollers can reap significant benefits. The key is knowledge. Virtually every casino has its own unique system of comps. When checking into the casino or applying for your slot club card, find out about what is available for your level of play. Ask for informational materials. Especially useful are charts or tables that indicate how points are credited and the number of points that will be needed in order to qualify for a desired comp. Most importantly, if you are planning to spend some time in the casino, ask about possible discounts that you might qualify for during your stay. Many comp systems are so complex and have so many possible benefits that they will not even be mentioned to you unless you ask. Don't be shy about asking.

Generally speaking, the face value of comps that a casino will award a customer will be 30% to 40% of the amount that the casino expects the customer to lose in the casino. This, however, does not mean that the casino will return to the customer 30 to 40% of the customer's losses because comps are almost always in the form of goods and services that will be accounted for by the casino at the casino "sell" price. For example, if a $30 show ticket is awarded to a customer, it will be recorded by the casino as a $30 comp. However, if the show had not been sold out

*A "pit boss" manages the dealers in a designated area of the casino known as a "pit" where table games are in operation.

and the recipient of the show ticket would not otherwise have attended the show, there would have been no actual cost to the casino. Nevertheless, since both parties to such transactions will usually be happy with the result, such comps are usually a win-win situation for both the casino and the casino patron. There is, however, usually one additional benefit of such things as comped meals and rooms. If there is a waiting list, in most casinos, customers who are being comped are given VIP treatment and are moved to the head of the line.

At this point, a cautionary note is in order. As was indicated earlier, casinos issue comps based on the amount that the casino expects to earn from the customer. It is only because the casino expects to win more from the high roller than the low roller that the casino gives the more valuable comps to the high roller. Therefore, it is not logical to increase the size of your bets in order to qualify for more valuable comps, because the increase in the value of the comps that you might earn will almost always be more than offset by an increase in the amount that you will probably lose. In other words, your pursuit of comp points should not be driven by the thought of winning something; it should be driven by the thought of minimizing the cost of your entertainment. There is one possible exception. If you are on the verge of qualifying for a valuable comp, such as a free room or a heavily discounted room and you do not have much time, it might be worthwhile to temporarily increase the size of your bets. Most casinos have electronic card readers located throughout the casino where patrons can check on their point total. Also, almost any casino employee can help you get information on your current comp point total. Again, don't be shy about asking for information about how you might be able to save a little money.

Eligibility for a comp is based on the total points that have been credited to an account. It is therefore usually advantageous for a married couple to have all their play credited to a common account. This can be done by getting two cards issued to their common account because in this way, it will be possible for both husband and wife to earn credits simultaneously while playing on different machines or in different parts of the casino. Upon request, many casinos have no qualms about issuing more than two cards on an account, even for customers who are not even related. At other casinos, eligibility for a room rate discount will be determined based on the total number of credits that were earned by all occupants of the room. The point is that virtually every casino has its own unique system of comps. Therefore, in order to insure that you get all that you are entitled to, be prepared to ask about what can be done to maximize your potential for earning comp credits.

From a modest beginning some sixty years ago as a case-by-case program designed to pamper and flatter a few select high rollers, casino comps have grown into a complex industry within an industry about which entire books have been written. Two of the best of these books are *The Frugal Gambler* and *More Frugal Gambler*, both by Jean Scott who frequently appears in the Discovery channel and Travel channel programs on the subject of gaming and was once dubbed the "Queen of Comps" by Dan Rather on the CBS news magazine *48 Hours*. For anyone who might be interested in a comprehensive coverage of casino comps, I highly recommend these books.

Casino Coupons

American consumers are the undisputed coupon-clipping champions of the world. Browse between the shelves of any American supermarket and you will probably spot some gray-haired elderly woman shifting through a fistful of coupons. Yet, for reasons unknown, this expertise is all too often grossly underutilized when the American consumer checks into a casino and fails to even look through the pack of coupons that can be found in every room of the casino. In addition to the coupons that are left in hotel rooms, there are usually potentially valuable coupons to be found in freebie newspapers and magazines that are located in various areas of the casino, particularly near the bell captain's stand. In addition to saving you money directly, these coupons can also help you stretch comp credits that you will earn while in the casino. Why waste comp credits that you will earn to get one free entry into the buffet if you and your spouse can use a 2-for-1 coupon that was left in your room?

Casino coupons come in all sizes and shapes. Many casinos issue "fun books" to guests when they check into the hotel. Fun books are packets of coupons that can only be used in that casino and are designed to discourage guests from wandering off to a competitor.

Probably the most popular casino coupons are the 2-for-1 buffet coupons. Casino managers favor buffet coupons because there is little labor involved in providing buffet service. Such facilities can therefore operate economically when business is slow, but can also readily accommodate a sudden surge in patronage. Another factor is that casino management has long been aware of the fact that everyone must eat. For this reason, 2-for-1 coupons for regular restaurant style meals are also very popular. However, such meal coupons should be read carefully before attempting to utilize them because many have time restrictions such as the time of the day or the day of the week when they may be used. Others are limited to use for specific meals such as breakfast or lunch.

For the typical casino guest who is on an extended stay, probably the most valuable coupons are the 2-for-1 night room coupons. These coupons give guests who pay for one night a second night free of charge. However, almost all these coupons have some restrictions. For example, many are not valid for Fridays, Saturdays, and holidays. Others require that reservations be made in advance or require that the coupons be presented at the time of check-in. This presents a problem because it requires that the guest have possession of the coupon before arriving at the casino.

There is a possible solution. The *Las Vegas Advisor*, a monthly subscription newsletter, provides much useful information on upcoming shows and events, as well a list of the top ten Las Vegas values in entertainment and dining. With each annual subscription, the *Las Vegas Advisor* provides the subscriber with a packet of coupons. Included among a seemingly endless variety of coupons in the packet are potentially valuable coupons for accommodations at several famous Las Vegas casinos. Potential savings from the use of these coupons alone can greatly exceed the cost of the subscription. However, for anyone who might be willing to move to a different hotel during the course of their stay in Las Vegas, in some cases, little further than across the street, the savings can be much greater.

Another popular type of coupon is the match-play coupon. With the match-play coupon, the casino matches bets for the player, usually to a maximum of $10. In other words, if a player bets $10, and uses a $10 match-play coupon, the casino will pay off a winning bet as if the player had actually bet $20. Therefore, if the player wins an even money bet while using a $10 coupon, he will receive $30. (The house retains the coupon.) This means that if a player uses a $10 coupon on a one-number roulette bet that normally pays off at 35 to one, he might expect to receive $710 ($350+$350+$10) on a winning $10-bet. Cognizant of the fact that the winner of such a bet will frequently "hit and run," most casinos limit use of match-play coupons to games such as blackjack, that usually pay even money on winning bets. Other casinos permit use of match-play coupons at any table game, but state in fine print that the winning bettor will be paid an additional $10. Beware of the fine print!

There are also coupons that supplement bets for a smaller amount. The most common of these coupons are the 7-5 coupons that are often referred to as "lucky bucks." Lucky bucks are most frequently found in fun books. With the 7-5 lucky buck, a $5 bet is treated as a $7 bet. Because of the lower risk of becoming a victim of a "hit and run," most casinos allow use of these coupons at any table game. However, as always, it pays to read the fine print.

Security in a Casino

In days now long gone, husky, unsmiling young men who looked like they had just stepped out of what was then known as a barbell club provided security within a casino. They were usually dressed in shinny black suits with loose-fitting jackets that everyone knew concealed a loaded weapon. By design, they were prominent figures in the casino, and the casino did nothing to discourage the notion that if displeased, these men were capable of inflicting serious physical damage in the parking lot.

Casino security today is far subtler and technically advanced. The security personnel that you are likely to encounter in a modern casino will probably consist of a few neatly dressed, uniformed personnel in key areas of the facility, and a smaller number of pleasant young men in stylish blazers who can be seen occasionally circulating about in the gaming area. However, the heart of the modern security system is nowhere in sight. It consists of cameras hidden away in the ceiling and a little-noticed room in the far reaches of the casino that is filled with banks of video screens that might extend from the floor to the ceiling. Constantly monitoring these screens will be casually dressed security personnel who have the ability to focus the cameras in on any slot machine, gaming table, cashier's cage or other potentially sensitive area of the casino. Any sign of a problem and a signal from one of these monitors could have a score of security personnel from throughout the casino converging on the area of concern almost instantly.

Except when in a restroom or in the privacy of a rented room, a casino guest should assume that he is under observation. However, unless he is engaged in some illegal activity, this should be of little concern because casinos are scrupulous in protecting the privacy of their guests; hence the saying that "What goes on in Las Vegas stays in Las Vegas."

The primary focus of casino security is the protection of guests from the petty thieves and scam artists who seem to abound in casinos. Most of these people are pathetic individuals who have lost all their money and are just trying to get back into action so that they can win their money back. It is safe to assume that none of these poor souls have ever read this book. Others, especially in places like Atlantic City and Las Vegas where there are large concentrations of casinos, are career petty thieves who prey on tourists for a living. A favorite trick of these scoundrels is to "accidentally" spill a drink on an unsuspecting tourist; then, while distracting the victim by feigning concern and apologizing profusely, an accomplice steals chips from the victim's chip rack or walks off with the victim's purse or wallet. There are minor variations to this ploy that are too numerous to mention. However, a couple of favorites are starting what appears to be a minor fracas in the casino or spilling a rack containing a few small denomination chips on the floor.

In general, security in most casinos is excellent today. However, you should always be alert. Never drink to excess. Avoid getting overly friendly with strangers, especially if you have just collected on a big payoff. Never accept a big payout in cash. The casino will always be happy to issue you a check or open a player's account for you. The real key to your security in a casino is always your own common sense.

Another concern for casino security personnel are players who try to surreptitiously increase the size of his bet after he has seen his cards, or tries to exchange cards with another player at the table. There is also the need to insure that a dealer does not try to sneak chips into his pockets during the course of the action or give an excessive amount of change to a friend. Regardless of the amount of experience that he might have had, no employee in casino security has seen it all because from time to time, some innovative shyster will come up with a new wrinkle.

Tipping in a Casino

Like their brethren in other segments of the service industry, casino employees are paid rather poorly and must therefore rely on tips, which are referred to in the industry as "tokes," in order to make ends meet. Therefore, casino employees such as bellboys, room cleaning women, and waitresses should be toked consistent with what would be appropriate outside of the casino. In other words, if the service was good, at least a small toke is always appropriate.

For employees who are engaged directly in a gaming activity, there are slightly differing practices for each activity. A keno runner who is giving good service should be toked whether you are winning or losing. If, as is customary, you are making a series of small bets, rather than toking when each bet is made, an occasional toke of a dollar or two should be adequate. If you score a big win, an additional toke would be appropriate when the keno runner brings you your winnings. If your wager was placed directly with the ticket writer, your toke should go to the ticket writer.

When playing a slot machine or a video poker machine, it is customary for winners, but not losers, to toke attendants. In most casinos, it will be necessary for an attendant to come and verify a jackpot. Usually however, because almost all slot machines now deal in vouchers that are taken to a cashier's cage or change machine for actual payment, there are few attendants to be found in the area of the machines. It might therefore be necessary to hunt down an attendant who had been especially helpful. However, if you have had a run of good luck, that attendant will always be most appreciative of your effort. In such cases, a toke of 2% to 5% of the amount that you won would probably be reasonable.

For table games, some casinos allow their dealers to keep their own tokes. However, in most casinos, tokes are now pooled and shared by all dealers within the same area. Casinos generally favor this pooling of tokes because it minimizes management problems about such things as who will be assigned to deal at a favored table. It is also thought to promote camaraderie among dealers and encourage them to cooperate in creating a pleasant, friendly atmosphere that will be beneficial to the casino as well as the dealers.

A toke to a dealer is usually made by flipping him a chip after he has dealt you a big winner. Examples are a poker hand that wins a large pot or a big winner such as a straight flush in "Let It Ride," which is a table game explained in Chapter 7. The practice of flipping the dealer a chip is also sometimes followed when a dealer who has been especially helpful or friendly rotates to a different table, when a player decides to leave the table, or a player goes on a roll and wins several consecutive hands. The amount of such tokes generally depends on the table limit and the size of the smallest denomination chips on the table. For games such as poker or keno, where there are many small denomination chips in use, a toke of one or more of these chips is usually adequate. If in doubt about the appropriate size of a toke, take notice of how much the other players at your table are toking.

Some players like to toke a dealer by placing a small bet for the dealer. If this is done, the dealer will have a stake in seeing the player win, which some believe to be advantageous. In general, dealers prefer the direct toke because they are not in the casino to gamble; they are there trying to make a living. This raises a closing thought on tokes. You are in the casino because you want to relax and enjoy yourself. Casino employees are there because they are trying to make a living. Therefore, if you were treated well and you enjoyed yourself, whether you won or lost, a toke is both fair and appropriate.

The Compulsive Gambler

The overwhelming majority of adult Americans participate in some form of gambling on a regular basis. This may be as innocuous as the weekly church bingo game or a small office football pool. A relatively small percentage of these gamblers become severely addicted to gambling. However, it has been long recognized that addiction to gambling can be as destructive to an individual and his loved ones as an addiction to alcohol or illicit drugs. In fact, addiction to gambling is now recognized as a mental disorder by the American Psychiatric Association.

Addiction to gambling usually develops slowly and insidiously. In the early stages, the addict will gradually begin to spend more and more time in the casino. Soon he will be failing to fulfill social commitments to family and friends. As the addiction progresses, he will periodically fail to show up for work. All the while, he will gradually begin to have financial difficulties and will sometimes tell lies in order to borrow money to feed his addiction. He may even resort to petty larceny or even more serious criminal activity.

Gamblers Anonymous, a nonprofit fellowship support group for compulsive gamblers, has developed the following series of twenty questions in order to help identify compulsive gamblers.

Did you ever lose time from work or school due to gambling?

Has gambling ever made your home life unhappy?

Has gambling affected your reputation?

Have you ever felt remorse about gambling?

Did you ever gamble to get money with which to pay debts or solve financial problems?

Did gambling cause a decrease in your ambition or efficiency?

After losing, did you feel you must return as soon as possible and win back your losses?

After winning, did you have a strong urge to return and win even more?

Did you often gamble until your last dollar was gone?

Did you ever borrow money to finance your gambling?

Have you ever sold anything to finance your gambling?

Were you ever reluctant to use "gambling money"- for normal expenditures?

Did gambling make you careless of the welfare of yourself or your family?

Did you ever gamble longer than you had planned?

Have you ever gambled to escape worry or trouble?

Have you ever committed or considered committing an illegal act to finance gambling?

Did gambling cause you to have difficulty sleeping?

Do arguments, disappointments or frustrations create within you an urge to gamble?

Did you ever have an urge to celebrate any good fortune by a few hours of gambling?

Have you ever considered self-destruction or suicide as a result of your gambling?

A "yes" response to seven or more of these questions is generally considered to be indicative of a potentially serious problem.

If you believe that you or a love one may have a problem with compulsive gambling, it is strongly recommended that you consider contacting the local chapter of Gamblers Anonymous, which will be listed in your local telephone directory. Gamblers Anonymous, which has more than 300 chapters in the United States, also has a website (http://www.GamblersAnonymous. org) where much useful information, including a listing of all active chapters worldwide can be found.

The Internal Revenue Service

The Oxford American College Dictionary defines winnings as "Money won, especially from gambling." Therefore, if you paid $300 in order to enter a poker tournament and survived long enough to qualify for payment of $600, you would probably assume that your winnings were $300. You would be wrong. The IRS, which apparently uses a different dictionary, has ruled that that in such an instance, your winnings were $600.

Gambling winnings (including the fair market value of non-cash prizes) are subject to Federal income taxes. At the end of the year, gambling losses may be deducted from winnings. However, the amount of such losses may not exceed the amount of winnings. A word of caution: although it is unequivocally clear that a non-cash prize that is won in a casino is subject to taxation, the meaning of "fair market value" is not. Never assume that the advertised value of a non-cash prize is the fair market value. For example, assume that you won a round-trip airline ticket to Hawaii that would normally have cost $500. However, at the time that you won the ticket, special off-season tickets were being advertised in the local newspaper for only $300. Provided that you are able to prove to the IRS that you could have purchased the ticket for only $300 by producing a copy of the advertisement, the IRS will undoubtedly accept the $300 figure as the actual value of your prize.

Tax codes are extremely complex and are sometimes subject to different interpretation, even within the IRS. If you have questions, consult a qualified tax consultant who specializes in questions that are related to gambling.

Because of differences in interpretation, the treatment of winnings in casinos may vary greatly between casinos. However, most casinos will issue the patron an IRS Form W-2G (Certain Gambling Winnings) in the following instances:

Keno Lounge: Form W-2G issued for winnings (reduced by the amount of the wager) of $1500 or more.

Bingo, Slot Machines, and Video Gaming Machines: Form W-2G issued for winnings (not reduced by the amount wagered) of $1200 or more. On slot and gaming machines, this is generally interpreted to apply to amounts won on any single play (spin) of the machine. Therefore, if a player accumulates credits totaling more than $1200, but no single payout was at least $1200, no Form W-2G will be issued. However, in most casinos, a Form W-2G will be issued if winnings total $5,000 or more, regardless of how the total was accumulated.

Poker Tournaments: Form W-2G issued whenever payment is $5,000 or more, regardless of the amount that was paid to enter the tournament.

Other Gaming Venues: Form W-2G issued whenever winnings are $5,000 or more.

Knowledge about when the casino will issue you a form W-2G can be extremely important to taxpayers who normally use the standard deduction when preparing their tax return because gambling losses can be deducted from winnings only if expenses are itemized on the tax return. This means that taxpayers who normally use the standard deduction will have the following options at the end of the year:

Option 1: Report winnings on Form 1040 and offset all or part of the winnings by itemizing losses on Schedule A.

Option 2: Report winnings on Form 1040, but continue to use the standard deduction. The net effect will be that the total amount of the winnings will be treated as taxable income.

The decision on which option you should use can be best made by preparing your tax return in draft form, utilizing each option and then using the most favorable option to actually file your return. Although this can be a nuisance, if you had significant gambling winnings that were reported to the IRS during the year and had been a borderline standard deduction tax filer, it might be well worth your while to consider your options.

In the event that you may choose to itemize your deductions, it is strongly recommended that you maintain a record of your gambling sessions. As a minimum, this record should include the following data:

Date of session
Name of casino (or casinos)
Approximate time of day
Game or games played
Total amount of money committed (buy-ins)
Total amount that was cashed in
Total amount won or lost for the day

Record the names of any witnesses, particularly dealers who might have been on duty. Also, keep any receipts that you might have received that day, such as parking receipts, valet checks or receipts for entering tournaments. Things like receipts for parking and valet checks are no proof that you suffered any losses, but they will tend to help verify that you were in the casino on the day that you had indicated.

If you use a slot card when playing one of the slot machines or video gaming machines, the casino has a record of how much you bet and how much you had cashed out. Upon request, most casinos will provide you with a copy of this record which should help you document your losses for the year. However, the casino will probably have few useful records to help you document losses at table games.

Except possibly for bragging purposes, an IRS Form W-2G is of little value to the average casino gambler. In order to minimize the possibility of having this form issued to you, learn about the circumstances that will lead to having this form issued. In general, you will learn that most casino employees will be forthright and helpful in giving you this information. After all, they have nothing to gain by reporting you to the IRS, but are interested in pleasing their customers. Also, the Form W-2G is a nuisance to them as well as to you. In fact, in some casinos, slot machine jackpots that would normally be $1200 or only slightly higher are set at slightly below $1200 in order to avoid the necessity of issuing a Form W-2G.

There are a variety of steps that you can take to avoid having a Form W-2G issued to you. If you have accumulated machine credits or gaming chips totaling close to the level that will trigger a W-2G, consider cashing out and taking a break. There are usually a variety of things to do in and around a casino—such as shopping, swimming, or dining. After your break, start over with a smaller amount if you still want to play. It is known that in some cases, casino guests have avoided a W-2G by playing down machine credits before cashing in or dividing a stack of chips and cashing in a portion of the chips on the following day. If done discreetly for reasonable amounts, such measures are not likely to result in complications because casino employees have nothing to gain by blowing the whistle. The key is discretion. Don't throw your money around. Be pleasant. Leave a decent toke.

Part I

Classic Table Games

Baccarat

Blackjack

Craps

Roulette

Mini-Baccarat Table Layout

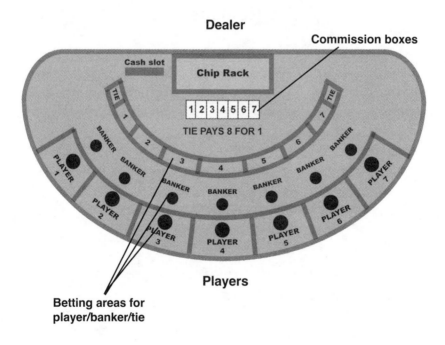

Dealer

Commission boxes

Cash slot

Chip Rack

1 2 3 4 5 6 7

TIE PAYS 8 FOR 1

Players

Betting areas for player/banker/tie

2. Baccarat

Because it is one of the easiest casino games to understand and play well, baccarat is the ideal subject for this first discourse on casino games. In fact, the only thing that the novice need know in order to play the game as well as any seasoned veteran is to avoid betting on a tie. The game is also attractive because it offers the novice one of the best (least unfavorable) overall odds in the casino. Baccarat is therefore probably the game that gives the average recreational casino visitor the best chance of leaving the casino with more money in his pocket than when he entered. That is probably the reason why, although the game has enjoyed considerable popularity in Europe and Asia, baccarat has never been enthusiastically promoted in American casinos.

In most American casinos, baccarat is played at a small table with only one casino employee at the table. This American version of the game is usually referred to as mini-baccarat. In a small number of American casinos, the game is also played at a full-size European style table that is essentially two mini-baccarat tables connected by a panel at which a coupier (dealer) and one or two assistants are stationed. In general, betting limits at a full-size table are higher. Otherwise, playing rules are identical.

Rules of Baccarat

After bets have been made, the game begins with the dealer dealing two hands consisting of two cards each from a card rack (known as a shoe) which contains six to eight decks of cards. The first and third cards go to a hand that is designated as the Player

Hand. The second and fourth cards go to a hand designated as the Banker Hand.

The object of the game is to make a hand that totals nine. For counting purposes, cards have the following values. Suits are not relevant.

Card Values for Baccarat

Card	Numerical Value
Ace	One
2	Two
3	Three
4	Four
5	Five
6	Six
7	Seven
8	Eight
9	Nine
10, Jack, Queen & King	Zero

If the total of the first two cards is greater than nine, the first digit is disregarded. For example, if the first two cards are a five and a six, the numerical value of the hand will be one (5+6 = 11).

After the first two cards have been dealt to the Player Hand and the Banker Hand, the dealer will automatically complete play based on established procedures. Neither the dealer nor player has an option. Provided that the Banker Hand is not an eight or nine, the dealer will complete the Player Hand in accordance with the following rules.

Action on the Player Hand

First Two Card Total	Player Hand Will
0, 1, 2, 3, 4, 5	Receive an additional card
6 or 7	Stand pat
8 or 9	Stand pat (Natural)

If the Player Hand is a nine and the Banker Hand is not a nine, the Player Hand is an automatic winner. If the Banker Hand is also a nine, it is a push and bets are returned.

If the Player Hand is an eight and the Banker Hand is nine, the Player Hand loses. If the Banker Hand is also an eight, it is a push. In summary, if the first two cards of either the Player Hand or the Banker Hand totals eight or nine, no additional cards will be dealt to either hand.

If the first two cards of the Player Hand totals six or seven and the Banker Hand does not total eight or nine, the Banker Hand will be completed by the dealer in accordance with the following procedure.

Action on Banker Hand—I

Banker Hand Total	Banker Hand Will
0, 1, 2, 3, 4, 5	Draw a card
6, 7, 8, 9	Stand pat

If the Player Hand has been given a third card, the dealer will act on the Banker Hand in accordance with the following rules.

Action on Banker Hand—II

Banker Hand Total	Banker Hand Will
0, 1, 2	Always draw a card
3	Draw, except if third card to Player Hand is 8
4	Draw, except if third card to Player Hand is 0, 1, 8 or 9
5	Draw, except if third card to Player Hand is 0, 1, 2, 3, 8 or 9
6	Draw, except if third card to Player Hand is 0, 1, 2, 3, 4, 5, 8 or 9
7	Never draw a card

The Betting

Minimum and maximum bets are posted at each table. Because of the small house advantage on this game, normally $25 is the smallest bet that will be accepted at a mini-baccarat table. At full-size baccarat tables, the minimum bet is usually $100. Patrons may bet on either the Player Hand or the Banker Hand. They may also bet that the two hands will tie.

The rules of baccarat have been designed to give the Banker Hand a slight (1.4%) advantage over the Player Hand. Therefore, in order to insure that the casino will have the necessary house advantage over the patron, regardless of how he might wish to bet, a 5% commission (or vigorish) is charged whenever the patron bets on the Banker Hand and wins his bet. This means that if the patron wins a $100 bet on the Player Hand, he will win $100. However, for a winning bet on the Banker Hand, he will win only $95. The net result is that the casino enjoys a very reasonable 1.2% advantage on bets that are made on the Banker Hand. In summary, the casino enjoys a 1.4% advantage over the patron if he is betting on the Player Hand and a 1.2% advantage if he is betting on the Banker Hand. The difference of 0.2% amounts to five cents on a minimum $25 bet.

In most casinos, the payout on a bet that the two hands will tie is 8 to 1. Since the true odds that the two hands will tie is 9.5 to 1, the house advantage on this bet is almost 15%, making this one of the worst bets in the casino. Therefore, in every book on this subject that I have read, it is strongly recommended that you never bet that the hands will tie. This writer makes no such recommendation. The vast majority of casino visitors are occasional patrons who are in the casino to relax and have some fun. There are times in every gambler's life when everything seems to be going his way and he senses that he can beat all odds and whip all comers. If such is the case and you understand the odds, I see no harm in making an occasional long-shot bet. Just don't make a habit of it and don't bet the family farm on it.

Closing Notes

The typical wording on a mini-baccarat table indicates that a winning tie bet will pay "9 for 1." Don't be misled. That note means that the winning bettor will receive $9 for each $1 that had been bet. However, since the $9 will include the $1 that had been wagered, payment will actually be made for odds of 8 to 1. The lesson here is that "9 for 1" is not synonymous with "9 to 1;" it is synonymous with 8 to 1. This is true not just at a baccarat table, but throughout the casino. When in a casino, always bear in mind that "X for 1" is not the same as "X to 1."

At most baccarat tables, you will notice that the table is cluttered with tab sheets on which players are keeping records of previous results. A wide variety of symbols will be used to record Player Hand wins, Banker Hand wins, and ties. Apparently, the object is to detect trends that might help the player intelligently size future bets. However, since as when flipping a coin, each baccarat hand is totally independent of previous results, such data is totally worthless. Nevertheless, casinos seem pleased to help perpetuate the myth that such data might be useful by providing free tab sheets and pencils. In fact, many casinos provide players this same information on an electronic sign that is located behind each table.

Blackjack Table Layout

Dealer

Discards   Cash slot   Chip Rack   Shoe   Bet Levels
Min $5
Max $100

BLACKJACK PAYS 3 TO 2

Dealer must stand on 17 and must draw to 16

INSURANCE • PAYS • 2 TO 1

Betting Circle

Insurance Bets

Players

3. Blackjack

Aside from poker, which is the only casino game in which the player does not compete directly against the house, blackjack is the only game in the casino that has been proven to be beatable over an extended period of time. This will be discussed in some detail later in this chapter.

The object of blackjack is to beat the dealer by making a hand that has a point total that is higher than the dealer's hand. However, the point total must not exceed twenty-one. For counting purposes, cards are accorded values as indicated in the table that follows.

Card Values for Blackjack

Card	Value of Card
Ace	One or eleven, *(whichever is more advantageous)*.
2 through 9	Number shown on the card.
10, Jack, Queen & King	Ten

After bets have been made, play begins with the dealer giving each player, as well as herself, two cards, beginning with the player to her left. One of the dealer's cards will be dealt face-up. Cards to players will be dealt face-up or face-down. If the dealer's exposed card is an Ace or a card with a value of ten, she will check her down card to see if she has a "natural" (two cards that add up to a point total of 21). If she does have a natural, she will beat all players, except for any players who also have a natural, who will "push" (tie the dealer).

If the dealer does not have a natural, she will make payment at 3 to 2 to any player who has a natural and then turn her attention to the player who is seated to her immediate left (who is commonly referred to as the first baseman). Each player, in turn, will then be given the option to "hit" (take an additional card) or "stand pat" (take no additional cards). If a player who has taken an additional card goes over twenty-one, he is said to have "busted" and is an automatic loser. The dealer will therefore pick up that player's cards as well as the chips that he had been wagering.

After acting on each player's hand, the dealer will act on her own hand in accordance with established procedures. If after completing action on her hand, the point total of her hand exceeds twenty-one, any player who has a hand that does not exceed twenty-one is an automatic winner.

If the dealer has not busted, the point total of the dealer's hand will be compared to the point total of each player's hand, and the hand with the higher total will be the winner. If the point totals are identical it will be a push.

Novices in a casino are sometimes taken aback to see that the dealer is allowed to see a player's hand before acting on her own hand. Actually, this is in no way adverse to the player's chances because the dealer is required to act on her hand in accordance with established procedure. For example, if a player stands on a hand that totals 15 because the dealer's exposed card is a 6, the dealer will be required to hit even if her point total is 16 and the dealer already has the player beat. In fact, exposing the cards of all players is beneficial to any player who might be counting cards.

Although house rules may vary somewhat between casinos, in the vast majority of casinos, the dealer will be required to hit (take an additional card) if she has:

- A hand in which her point total is 16 or less.
- A hand in which she has an Ace and, counting the Ace as an 11, her point total is 17 or less.

These rules apply regardless of the number of cards that are in the dealer's hand. For example, if the first two cards in the dealer's hand had been a nine and a three, and her third card had been a four, she would be required to take another card because the point total of her three cards would then be only 16 (9+3+4).

Blackjack originally began as a game that was played with a single deck of cards. However, most blackjack games are now played utilizing a shoe that contains four to six decks. Among the reasons for this change are efficiency and security. The multiple-deck game is more efficient because it speeds up play by reducing down time while the cards are being shuffled. It is also more secure because it makes it more difficult to count cards. Recently, some casinos have begun to install continuous shuffle machines, which further increases efficiency and makes card counting an exercise in futility.

There is a further benefit that a multiple-deck game gives the house that is not readily apparent to the average casino patron. Use of the multiple deck makes it slightly more difficult to make a natural, and because the casino must pay 3 to 2 to players who have a natural, the fewer naturals that appear, the better for the casino. In order to explain why it is more difficult to make a natural in a multiple-deck game than in a single-deck game, a simple explanation follows.

Regardless of the number of decks in use, the probability of getting an Ace on the first card will be one in thirteen because the number of decks in use does not affect the ratio of aces to the other cards in the deck (or decks).

If the first card is an Ace, completing the natural requires a 10, Jack, Queen, or King. If one card (the first Ace) is taken out of the deck, there will be 51 cards remaining. If a card is taken from a packet containing two decks, there will be 103 cards remaining in the packet, etc. Since there are a total of sixteen 10s, Jacks, Queens and Kings in each deck, the probability of completing a natural is summarized in the next table.

Probability of Completing a Natural

Number of Decks	Probability
One deck	16/51 = 31.37%
Two decks	32/103 = 31.07%
Three decks	48/155 = 30.97%
Four decks	64/207 = 30.92%

When acting on his hand, in addition to deciding to hit or stand pat, the player will have the following additional options:

(a) The player may opt to double his wager (double-down). In general, this option will be offered only if the first two cards total ten or eleven. If this option is exercised, the player will receive only one additional card. If the first two cards were dealt face-up, the third card will be dealt face-up. If the first two cards were dealt face-down, these two cards will be turned face-up and the third card will be dealt face-down.

(b) The player may opt to split his first two cards and play them as two separate hands with each hand being played for the amount of the original wager. In most casinos, this option is available only if the first two cards are paired. However, in some casinos, this option is available if the first two cards are of equal value. For example, it might be permissible to split a Jack and a King because both cards have a value of ten. However, it would be a very bad play to split a Jack and a King because a hand with a point total of twenty is a very strong hand. Why break up a strong hand in order to create two possible disasters? Incidentally, if ten-value cards are split and an Ace is received, that does not constitute a natural that will pay 3 to 2. It will be treated as an ordinary "21."

Cards that were dealt face-down will be turned face-up and the dealer will place one card on the first of the two cards. The player will then decide to hit or stand pat. After completing play on this first hand, the dealer will place a card on the second hand, and that hand will be played in the normal manner. If an additional card again pairs one of the cards that was originally split, the player will be given an option to split further and play a third hand for an additional bet. The exception is if the cards that were split were Aces. If Aces were split, the player will be given only one additional card on each Ace and may not split further.

Bets are made by placing chips in the small circles on the table in front of each player's seat. Minimum and maximum bets that are allowed at the table are always shown on the table. Once the dealer has begun to deal out the cards, do not touch the chips that are in the circle.

If the cards were dealt to you face-up, do not touch your cards. Indicate that you wish to hit by making a scratching motion with your fingers. Indicate that you wish to stand by waving your hand palm-down over your cards.

If the cards were dealt to you face-down, indicate that you wish to hit by scratching the table with your cards. Indicate that you wish to stand by sliding your cards under the chips that you had wagered. Use only one hand to pick up your cards.

Blackjack is currently being played with such a wide variety of house rules that it would be difficult to describe more than a few of the more common ones. In fact, in many casinos, different rules apply to different tables within the same casino. For example, in some casinos, high-limit games are played with only one deck of cards, but multiple decks are used for lower limit games. Also, dealers are required to stand on "soft seventeen" at some tables but are required to hit a soft seventeen at other tables. Incidentally, a "soft seventeen" is a hand in which at least one of the cards is an Ace that may be counted as a one or as an eleven. Therefore, the hand cannot be busted if an additional card is drawn. For example, a hand that consists of an Ace and a six is a soft seventeen and a hand that consists of a king and a seven is a "hard" seventeen. In fact, any hand with an Ace that is not a natural is referred to as a "soft" hand. Hands without Aces are referred to as "hard" hands.

Because it is not practical to prepare playing recommendations for a virtually endless variety of rules, playing recommendations contained in this chapter are based on what is believed to be the most common elements of the typical casino blackjack table.

Therefore, the playing recommendations that follow are based on the assumption that the these basic rules are applicable:

- A natural will pay 3 to 2.
- Dealer must hit when she has a hard sixteen, but must stand if she has a hard seventeen.
- Dealer must hit soft seventeen but stand on soft eighteen.
- Players may double-down only when the first two cards total ten or eleven.
- Only pairs may be split.

If Aces had been split, only one additional card is allowed and the hand may not be further split if another Ace appears. If a card with a value of ten is received, this will not be considered to be a natural but as a normal hand with a value of 21. Similarly, if cards with a value of ten had been split and an Ace appears, it will be treated as a normal 21 rather than as a natural.

Basic Blackjack Playing Strategy

In blackjack, the house advantage is based largely on the fact that the player must act on his hand before the dealer acts on her hand. Therefore, the player may bust before the dealer acts. This huge house advantage is only partially offset by such player advantages as the 3 to 2 payoff for naturals and the option to split pairs. It is therefore extremely important to exercise the hit or stand options wisely.

The following table, which is the result of various computer studies, shows the percentage of times that a dealer will go bust based on her exposed card.

Dealer Bust Percentage

Dealer's Exposed Card	Bust Percentage
2	35%
3	37%
4	40%
5	43%
6	42%
7	26%
8	24%
9	23%
10, Jack, Queen, or King	21%
Ace	11%

Note that the dealer's bust percentage is very high if she is showing a 4, 5, or 6, but that it declines dramatically if her exposed card is 7. The reason is that if her exposed card is 7 or higher, there is a high probability that she will not be hitting. In that situation, therefore, there is an incentive for players to hit when their first two cards total less than seventeen.

In view of the foregoing, the following tables were prepared in order to provide the reader with basic playing strategy based on the first two cards that he has received.

Strategy for Hard Hands

Your Hand	Action
17 or more	Always stand pat.
12 thru 16	Hit except if dealer's card is 2, 3, 4, 5, or 6.
11	Double-down except if dealer's card is an Ace.
10	Double-down except if dealer's card is Ace, 10, or face card.
Less than 10	Hit.

Strategy for Soft Hands

Your Hand	Action
Ace-8, Ace-9	Stand pat.
Ace-7	Double-down if dealer's card is 2, 3, 4, 5 or 6; Stand if dealer's card is 7 or 8; Hit if dealer's card is 9, 10, or Ace.
Ace-6	Hit if dealer's card is 2, 7, 8, 9, 10, or Ace; Double-down if dealer's card is 3, 4, 5, or 6.
Ace-5	Hit if dealer's card is 2, 3, 7, 8, 9, 10, or Ace; Double-down if dealer's card is 4, 5, or 6.
Ace-4	Hit if dealer's card is 2, 3, 7, 8, 9, 10, or Ace; Double-down if dealer's card is 4, 5, or 6.
Ace-2, Ace-3	Hit if dealer's card is 2, 3, 4, 7, 8, 9, 10, or Ace; Double-down if dealer's card is 5 or 6.

Strategy for Paired Hands

Your Hand	Action
Ace-Ace	Always split.
10-10	Never split.
9-9	Split unless dealer's card is an Ace or 10.
8-8	Always split.
7-7	Split if dealer's card is 2, 3, 4, 5, 6, or 7; Hit if dealer's card is 8, 9, 10, or Ace.
6-6	Split if dealer's card is 2, 3, 4, 5, or 6; Hit if dealer's card is 7, 8, 9, 10, or Ace.
5-5	Never split.

4-4	Hit if dealer's card is 2, 3, 4, 7, 8, 9, 10, or Ace; Split if dealer's card is 5 or 6.
3-3, 2-2	Split if dealer's card is 2, 3, 4, 5, 6, or 7; Hit if dealer's card is 8, 9, 10, or Ace.

After receiving your third card, apply the same strategy that is indicated in these tables. For example, if you had hit a hard 14 and received a deuce, making your new total 16, you should hit again. However, if your third card was a three, giving you a new total of 17, you should stand on your hard 17.

Insurance

Most casinos offer what is referred to as insurance at their blackjack tables. In casinos where insurance is offered, if the dealer's exposed card is an Ace, she will stop play and ask if any of the players would like to buy insurance against the possibility that the dealer has a natural. Insurance is a side bet that is made by placing chips in the area of the table that is marked "Insurance Pays 2 to 1." Usually, this side bet is limited to one half of the player's basic bet.

If the dealer does have a natural, players who had purchased insurance win two dollars for each dollar that was wagered on this side bet. However, since only four (10, Jack, Queen, and King) of the thirteen denominations will give the dealer a natural, almost all books on this subject conclude that insurance is a poor bet because essentially, the casino will be paying only 8 to 4 on true odds of 9 to 4.

Such a conclusion is overly simplistic and will sometimes result in a missed opportunity because the relevant ratio is the ratio of ten-valued cards remaining in the unused portion of the deck in relation to the smaller denomination cards remaining in the deck. For example, if at a table where a single deck is in use, there are thirteen cards showing on the first hand that was dealt, and none of the cards that are showing is a ten-valued card, the relevant ratio is not 16 to 36, but 16 to 23. Therefore, an insurance bet will have a significant positive expectation. In this regard, note that in the above example, even if two of the thirteen exposed cards are ten-valued cards, the relevant ratio will be 14 to 25, still resulting in a positive expectation. When seated at a blackjack table, be alert to such opportunities. Skill in counting cards will be helpful in spotting such situations, but in many cases, all that will be needed is a mind that is cognizant of the possibilities.

Surrender

In some casinos, players are given the option to surrender if they don't like their chances after looking at their first two cards and the dealer's exposed card. If the option to surrender is offered only after the dealer has checked to see if she has a natural, it is known as a late surrender. If the option is offered regardless whether the dealer has a natural, it is known as an early surrender. Obviously, the table that offers the early surrender option is more favorable to the player. Players surrender by telling the dealer that they wish to surrender and giving up one-half of the amount that they had originally wagered. The dealer will then pick up the player's cards and return half the amount of the player's bet. If this option is available, it is recommended that you surrender only under the following circumstances that are indicated in the Surrender Table.

Strategy for Surrender

Your Hand	Surrender If Dealer's Card Is:
Hard 16	Ace, King, Queen , Jack or 10
Hard 15	King, Queen, Jack or 10

Finding a Good Blackjack Table

Key factors affecting your chances of having a winning session at a blackjack table are the rules that are in effect at the table. Take note of the characteristics of the game, especially with regard to the following factors:

- **Number of decks in use.** The ideal game will have one deck in use. However, such games are sometimes hard to find except in very high-limit games. If there is more than one deck in use, the fewer decks the better.

- **Payout for naturals.** A 3 to 2 payout is the norm. Do not accept less. In rare instances, such as a promotion, a casino might offer a 2 to 1 payout. Don't miss out on such an opportunity.

- **Dealer hits hard 16, but stands on soft 17.** In most casinos, dealers hit soft 17. It would be advantageous to you (by a small margin), if the dealer stands on soft 17.

- **Double-down allowed after splitting pairs.** In some casinos, players are allowed to double-down after splitting a pair. This could be very advantageous if, for example, after splitting a pair of eights against the dealer's exposed five, you receive a two or a three on either or both of your eights.

- **Double-down allowed on soft hands.** It is beneficial for the player if he can use the double-down recommendations in the strategy table for soft hands. However, many tables only allow doubling on hard hands. If that is the case, the player should hit soft hands in the circumstances in which doubling is preferred, but not allowed.

Counting Cards

When the dealer prepares to deal from a freshly shuffled deck (or decks) of cards, the fraction of ten-valued cards (10, Jack, Queen and King) will always be 30.77% (16/52). However, as hands are dealt, this fraction will change. It has been mathematically proven that if this fraction increases sufficiently, the house advantage can become a player advantage. It has also been proven that an abundance of low cards (2, 3, 4, 5, and 6) in the unused portion of the deck increases the house advantage, but that an abundance of medium cards (7, 8 and 9) has no significant impact on the house advantage.

A deck that is abnormally rich in ten-value cards is advantageous for the player for the following reasons:

- It will result in an increase in the number of naturals that are dealt. Since players are paid 3 to 2 when they have a natural, but the dealer is not, this is a change that greatly favors the player. Obviously, an abundance of Aces in the unused portion of the deck will also result in an increase in the number of naturals.

- It will result in an increase in the number of hands that will bust. Since the dealer must hit hard hands that are prone to bust, the abundance of big cards in the deck is advantageous to the player.

- An abundance of ten-value cards enhances the value of the hand when a player doubles down.

Over the years, numerous systems have been developed in order to count the cards that remain in the unused portion of the deck. The most commonly used system is known as the high-low count (HLC) system. With the HLC system, the following points are assigned to cards and a continuous count is maintained of all cards that remain in the unused portion of the deck.

Points for Cards in the High-Low Count System

Cards	Point
2, 3, 4, 5 & 6	+1
7, 8 & 9	0
10, J, Q, K & Ace	-1

For an example, consider a first hand dealt that exposed the cards shown in the table. Each hand would have the net points shown in the last row.

High-Low Count Example

Player	#1	#2	#3	#4	#5	Dealer
Cards	J, 6, 5	7, 5, 4, 2	Q, 6	9, 4	3, 4, 8	4, 6, 10
Net Points	+1	+3	0	+1	+2	+1

The net count for the six hands in this example is +8. Since any positive number is a good sign for players, if only one deck is in use, it would be wise to increase the bet on the next hand. However, if eight decks were in use, the +8 count would be insignificant because that would be equivalent to a +1 count in a game in which only one deck is in use.

If you have an inclination to try your hand at counting cards, simply get a deck of cards and practice on your kitchen table. Deal out a series of hands to several imaginary players and practice until you are capable of maintaining an accurate continuous count through the entire deck. Obviously, at the end of the deck, your count should be zero. After you have acquired the skill to maintain an accurate count through one deck at the pace of a normal casino blackjack table, add one or two additional decks and continue practicing.

The object of the card counter is to get the edge on the house by betting small amounts when the house has the advantage and betting larger amounts when the player has the edge. However, bear in mind that casino employees have been trained to detect card counters. Therefore, skill is needed in order to minimize the possibility of being detected. If you have been betting the table minimum of $5 when a favorable condition develops, it would probably be unwise to suddenly increase your bet to the table maximum of $500 because this will most likely result in the dealer reshuffling the cards. In this regard, you should bear in mind that under the best of circumstances, a skillful card counter can only occasionally get a small temporary edge over the house. Therefore, for even the most skillful card counter, blackjack is not an easy road to wealth and fortune, but a sometimes tense, often tedious, day-to-day grind.

In his best selling book, *Bringing Down The House,* Ben Mezrich describes how a team of geeks from MIT won more than $3 million over a period of two years by traveling across the country and utilizing the HLC system. In order to minimize the possibility of detection, some members of the team served as spotters who would bet small amounts while counting cards. When a favorable condition developed, the spotter would continue to bet a small amount but would secretly signal another member of the team who just "happened to be in the area." This accomplice would then come to the table and bet large amounts of money.

There is nothing illegal or unethical about counting cards. Therefore, if you have the inclination, I would encourage you to teach yourself how to do so because this will equip you with something more than raw hunches about how to size your bets.

In the old days, when organized crime controlled gambling, if detected, a card counter could expect to be met by goons in the parking lot who would forcefully inform the card counter that his continued patronage would not be appreciated. In this day of benign corporate management, the invitation to take one's patronage elsewhere is likely to be more civil, but no less definitive. More likely, the dealer will probably simply be instructed to shuffle the deck more frequently. However, the widespread use of recently developed continuous shuffle machines is expected to make either recourse unnecessary.

Craps Table Layout

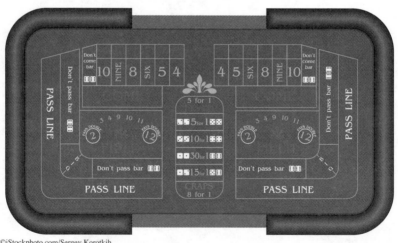

©iStockphoto.com/Sergey Korotkih

4. Craps

Craps is one of the oldest and most popular casino table games. It is also one of the easiest casino games to learn and understand. However, due to the complexity of the betting and the sometimes confusing, almost frantic pace of the action, many casino patrons are reluctant to give the game a try This is unfortunate because craps offers some of the best bets in the casino.

The game begins with one of the players (called the shooter) at the table throwing two die against a retaining wall. This first throw of the dice is called the "come out roll." If the total number of spots on the two die is 7 or 11 (which is referred to as a "natural"), the shooter wins his bet. If the total of the spots is 2, 3, or 12 (which is referred to as a "craps"), the shooter loses. In either case, the shooter is allowed to remain as the shooter and make another bet. However, he may also choose not to remain as the shooter and pass the dice to one of the other players at the table.

If the total of the dice on the come out roll is 4, 5, 6, 8, 9, or 10, that number becomes the shooter's "point" and the shooter will continue to roll the dice until he rolls either a 7 or his point. If the point appears before the 7, the shooter is said to have made a "pass." The shooter therefore wins his bet. If the 7 appears before the point, the shooter loses and the dice move to the next player.

Since there are six sides to each die, there are 36 possible combinations of the two die as is shown in the figure on the next page.

The 36 Possible Combinations for Two Six-Sided Die

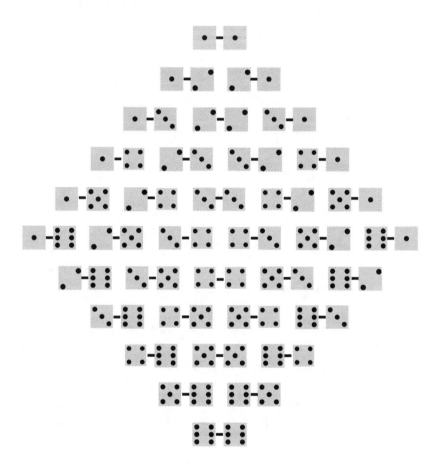

The possible combinations of the two die that are illustrated are summarized in the table. In many casinos, you will find players, especially the shooters, excitedly calling for their point to appear. I have therefore added commonly used nicknames for the various numbers.

Summary of Dice Combinations

Number	Common Nickname	Possible Combinations
2	Snake Eyes	1
3	Trey	2
4	Little Joe	3
5	Fever	4
6	Sixey from Dixie	5
7	Natural	6
8	Eighter from Decater	5
9	Kneener	4
10	Big Dick	3
11	Natural	2
12	Box Cars	1
Total Possible Combinations		36

Based on the data that is shown above, a few basic deductions can be made.

On the come out roll:

- There is a 22.2% (8 out of 36) chance that a natural will appear.
- There is a 11.1% (4 out of 36) chance that a craps will appear.
- There is a 66.7% (24 out of 36) chance that one of the six points will appear.

If the shooter has established a point:

- The shooter is a 5 to 6 underdog to win if his point is either 6 or 8. The reason is that there are six possible combinations that add up to 7, but only five combinations that add up to 6 or 8.
- The shooter is a 4 to 6 underdog to win if his point is 5 or 9.
- The shooter is a 1 to 2 (3 to 6) underdog to win if his point is 4 or 10.

The Pass Line Bet

The basic wager at a craps table is known as a "pass line bet." This is a bet that the shooter will win. This bet is made by placing chips in the section of the table that is marked "Pass Line." Although bettors may also bet that the shooter will lose (a don't pass bet), the pass line bet is by far the most commonly made bet at a craps table. Collectively, bets that will pay off if the shooter wins are known as "right bets" and bets that will pay off if the shooter loses are referred to as "wrong bets." On a pass line bet, the casino enjoys a 1.4% advantage over the bettor. However, as was noted above, on the come out roll, the shooter is twice as likely to win (throw a natural) as he is to lose (throw a craps). After a point has been established, however, the shooter is always an underdog.

The Odds Bet

After a shooter has established a point, the casino offers players who had made a pass line bet the opportunity to "take the odds" on an additional bet at true odds. In other words, if the shooter's point is 9, he will be allowed to make an additional bet at true odds of 2 to 3. This means that if the shooter takes odds on a $2 bet, he will win $3 on this second bet. He will, of course, also win his original bet. Since the casino gains no advantage on an odds bet, the net effect is that the house advantage on the total amount that was wagered on the pass line bet and the odds bet will decline. For example, if a player who had bet $10 on the pass line takes an odds bet for $10, the 1.4% house advantage on the original $10 bet will decline to approximately 0.85% on the combined total of $20. The more the bettor wagers on the odds bet, the more the house advantage will decline. Obviously, the house advantage can never decline to zero.

Because the casino enjoys no house advantage on an odds bet, only players who had made a pass line bet can make the bet. Also, the amount that may be wagered on an odds bet is contingent on the amount that was wagered on the pass line bet.

This amount varies between casinos, but is often limited to twice the amount that was wagered on the pass line bet.

When making an odds bet, it is necessary to size your bet properly in order to insure that the casino will be able to actually pay you true odds. For example, if you make a $5 odds bet when the point is 9, the casino might be unable to actually pay you true odds of $7.50 because the smallest chip on the table is a $1 chip. The easiest way to avoid any such complication is to make all odds bets in multiples of $10.

One interesting feature of the odds bet is that the bet may be withdrawn at the discretion of the bettor. The casino will have no objection because the casino enjoys no house advantage on an odds bet.

Another interesting feature of the odds bet is that the astute player can minimize the house advantage by properly apportioning the amount that he will wager between the pass line bet and the odds bet. For example, if the bettor wagers $20 on a pass line bet, the casino will enjoy a 1.4% advantage on the $20 wager. However, if the bettor wagers $10 on the pass line bet and then wagers an additional $10 on the odds bet after a point has been established, the house advantage on the total of $20 that was wagered will be only 0.85%. If he bets an additional $20 on the odds bet, the house advantage on the total of $30 will decline to 0.61%. However, as was indicated previously, casinos have limits on the amount that may be wagered on odds bets.

An odds bet is made by placing the amount of the bet just outside the pass line behind the amount that had been wagered on the pass line bet.

The Don't Pass Line Bet

The "don't pass line" bet is the opposite of the pass line bet and is a bet that the shooter will lose. However, in order to insure that the casino will have the necessary house advantage over don't pass line bettors, the 12 is a neutral number on the come out roll that results in tie. In order to minimize confusion, the following comparative table is provided.

Come Out Roll Summary

Number Rolled	Pass Line Bettor	Don't Pass Line Bettor
2	Loses	Wins
3	Loses	Wins
4, 5 & 6	Establishes Point	Establishes Point
7	Wins	Loses
8, 9 & 10	Establishes Point	Establishes Point
11	Wins	Loses
12	Loses	Ties

In some casinos, the 2 rather than the 12 is designated as the neutral number. This, however, does not affect the house advantage which is 1.4% over those who make a don't pass line bet.

Unlike the pass line bet which cannot be cancelled after a point has been established, a don't pass line bet may be cancelled. This is because after a point has been established, the don't pass bettor will have an advantage over the casino. Obviously, it would be foolish for any bettor to cancel a bet when the odds are in his favor.

Don't pass line bets are made by placing chips in the section of the table that is marked "Don't Pass Bar."

Laying Odds Bet

Once the shooter has established a point, players who have made a don't pass line bet may make a "laying odds bet" which is the opposite of the odds bet. In other words, the bettor will be wagering that the shooter will not be successful in making his point. Since the shooter will be an underdog to make his point, the laying odds bettor must give odds of $2 to $1 when the point is 4 or 10, $3 to $2 when the point is 5 or 9, and $6 to $5 when the point is 6 or 8. This means that like the odds bet, the casino will have no house advantage on a lay odds bet.

As when making an odds bet, in order to get full payment, it is necessary to wager the proper amount when making a laying odds bet. These amounts are as indicated in the following table.

Optimum Betting Amounts for Laying Odds Bets

Point	True Odds	Optimum Betting	Potential Winings
6 & 8	5 to 6	Multiples of $6	Multiples of $5
5 & 9	2 to 3	Multiples of $3	Multiples of $2
4 & 10	1 to 2	Multiples of $2	Multiples of $1

Since there is no space on the table to place a laying odds bet, tell the dealer that you wish to lay odds and he will place your bet partially atop the chips that you had wagered on the don't pass line bet. One of the reasons why there is no space provided on the table for laying odds bets is that relatively few players enjoy betting with the house against a fellow casino patron (the Shooter).

The pass line bet combined with the odds bet, and the don't pass line bet combined the laying odds bet, are among the best bets that are available in a casino. The bets also have the advantage of being very easy to understand and follow. There are numerous other types of bets that can be made at the craps table. Many of these other bets can be very confusing to a novice who may be lacking in experience at a craps table. It is therefore recommended that until you get acclimated, you limit yourself to the four types of bets that were discussed above.

The Place Bet

A "place bet" is a bet that the point (4, 5, 6, 8, 9, or 10) that a shooter had established will be rolled before the shooter rolls a 7. In essence, this is a bet on the shooter to win. Since a shooter who is trying to make a point is always an underdog, the casino will pay odds as indicated in the table that follows. Note, however, that the house will always pay less than true odds.

Place Bet Table

Point Number	True Odds	Payout Amount	Optimum Bet Amount.	House Advantage
6 & 8	5 to 6	$7 on $6 bet	Multiples of $6	1.5%
5 & 9	2 to 3	$7 on $5 bet	Multiples of $5	4.0%
4 & 10	1 to 2	$9 on $5 bet	Multiples of $5	6.6%

"Optimum Bet Amount" indicates how a place bet should be structured in order to insure that you will receive full payment on a winning bet. As is shown in the "House Advantage" column, place bets on 4, 5, 9, and 10 are rather costly when compared to bets that were discussed earlier. It is therefore recommended that a place bet be made only when the shooter's point is a 6 or 8.

In order to make a place bet, give your chips to the dealer and ask him to "place the six" (or whatever point you wish to bet). The attendant will then put your chips in the large box that is marked "Six."

The Buy Bet

Another way of betting that the shooter's point will appear before the 7 is known as the buy bet. This bet pays true odds. However, the casino charges a 5% vigorish (which is usually referred to as the "vig") on these bets. For example, a $20 bet that the 4 will be rolled before the 7 appears to pay $40, but the dealer must be given $21 before the bet will be accepted. Because of the 5% vigorish, buy bets should be made in multiples of $20 ($20, $40, $60, etc.).

Note that when the shooter's point is a 4 or 10, the house advantage on a buy bet is actually lower than on a place bet. However, when the shooter's point is 5, 6, 8 and 9, the house advantage is higher. Regardless, it is felt that the house advantage on all buy bets are too high and that these bets should therefore be avoided.

The Big 6 and Big 8 Bet

This is a third way to bet that either the 6 or the 8 will be rolled before the 7 appears. These bets pay even money and are made by placing chips in the box that is marked "Big 6" or "Big 8," as appropriate. Because the true odds are 6 to 5 against either the 6 or 8 appearing before the 7, the casino enjoys a huge 9.1% house advantage on these bets. Although there are other bets at the craps table that give the house an even bigger advantage, because basically the same bet can be made by making a place bet that gives the house only a 1.5% advantage, the Big 6 and Big 8 bets are in the opinion of the author, the "sucker bets" of the craps table. When at a craps table, stay away from any box that is marked "Big."

The Lay Bet

The lay bet is a bet that the 7 will be rolled before the shooter's point appears. It is, therefore, the opposite of the buy bet.

As with the buy bet, the casino pays true odds and charges a commission. However, because the vig is based on the amount that you stand to win rather than the amount that is being wagered, the house advantage on a lay bet is slightly lower than on a buy bet and varies with the point number as is indicated in the table.

Actual Vigorish on Lay Bets

Point Number	Vigorish
6 & 8	4.00%
5 & 9	3.22%
4 & 10	2.44%

Because the vig is lower on a lay bet than on a buy bet, the lay bet actually offers a better value. However, because most bettors prefer to bet with the shooter against the house rather than vice-versa, and because bettors are generally adverse to betting a relatively large amount in order to win a smaller amount, the buy bet is a far more popular bet in casinos than the lay bet.

The Hardway Bet

A "hardway bet" is a bet that may be made only when a shooter's point is a 4, 6, 8 or 10. This is a bet that the 4, 6, 8 or 10 will be rolled with a pair of deuces, threes, fours or fives before the shooter rolls a 7 or a 4, 6, 8 or 10 without pairing the two die. For example, if you bet the hardway 10, in order to win, the 5-5 combination must be rolled before any combination of 4-6, 1-6, 2-5 or 3-4 is rolled.

Bets are made by handing chips to one of the stickmen and telling him that you wish to make a hardway bet. He will place your wager in the appropriate box at the center of the table in the Hardway Bets section. Boxes in this section will indicate the amount that will be paid for winning bets.

The house advantage on a hardway bet when the point is a 4 or 10 is 11.1%. When the point is a 6 or 8, the house advantage is 9.1%. Hardway bets are, therefore, very poor bets that should be avoided.

The Come Bet

The "come bet" is a wager that runs parallel to a pass line bet but is otherwise identical to the pass line bet. A come bet may be made whenever a point has been established by the shooter. If a point has already been established, a large puck with "On" printed on a white surface will be located in the appropriate point box. If a point has not been established, the puck with "Off" printed on a black surface will be located elsewhere on the table. The next roll of the dice then services as the come out roll for the come bet. Because a come bet may be made before every roll after a point has been established, it can become very confusing for a novice. Hopefully, the table that follows will illustrate how the last come out roll impacts the pass line bet and any previous come bets.

Impact of Come Out Roll - Come Bet

Number Rolled	Last Come Bet	All Previous Bets
2	Loses	No impact
3	Loses	No impact
4, 5 & 6	Establishes point	See note*
7	Wins	Loses
8, 9 & 10	Establishes point	See note*
11	Wins	No impact
12	Loses	No impact

* If the come out roll on the last come bet is 4, 5, 6, 8, 9, or 10, it will have no impact on previous bets, except if the number that appeared is the point for one of the previous bets. In that case, the previous bettor will win his bet.

A come bet is made by placing chips in the large rectangular box that is marked "Come." If a point is established, an attendant will move the chips to the appropriately numbered box above the Come Box.

Because come bets frequently result in multiple overlapping bets, they are the primary reason why action at a craps table becomes so hectic and confusing for the novice craps player. So why was the come bet invented? The simple answer is profit for the casino. With the come bet, the number of currently outstanding bets at the table increases dramatically and the casino enjoys a house advantage on all bets except odds bets and laying odds bets which are neutral bets.

As with the pass line bet, players who have made a come bet and have established a point may take odds. Since all betting procedures are identical to that of the odds bet, the reader is referred to previous section on "The Odds Bet."

At this point, a word of caution is in order. After the dealer has paid off one of your winning bets, always be careful to remove your chips from the numbered and/or lettered portion of the table. Otherwise, it might be assumed that you had intended to parlay your bet.

The Don't Come Bet

The "don't come bet" is the opposite of the come bet and is a bet that the come bettor will lose. Therefore, except that the don't pass bet is based on the pass line bet and the don't come bet is based on the come bet, they are identical. I therefore refer the reader to the previous section on "The Laying Odds Bet."

All the bets that have been discussed above are collectively referred to as multiple-roll bets because unless a natural (7 or 11) or a craps (2, 3, or 12) appears on the next roll of the dice, additional rolls will be needed before the outcome of the bet can be determined. There are also several bets that will be determined on the first roll of the dice after a bet has been made. These bets are collectively referred to as one-roll bets and are discussed next.

The Field Bet

A "field bet" is a bet that 2, 3, 4, 9, 10, 11, or 12 will appear on the next roll of the dice. If a 2 or 12 is rolled, the bettor will receive $2 for each $1 that was wagered. The 3, 4, 9, 10, and 11 will pay even money. This is a very popular bet because with seven numbers that will win and only four that will lose, at first glance, it appears to be a good bet. In fact, because only sixteen of the thirty-six possible combinations of the dice are winners, but twenty are losers, the house will have a 5.26% advantage on the bet.

A field bet is made by placing your wager in the box that is prominently marked "Field."

Numbers Bet

A "numbers bet" is a wager that a 2, 3, 7, 11, 12 or any craps (2, 3 or 12) will appear on the next roll of the dice. This bet is made by giving the stickman your chips and telling him which bet you would like to make. He will put your bet in the appropriate box that shown in the diagram on page 46 that is between the two wings of the craps table. Pertinent data for a numbers bet is indicated in the table.

Numbers Bet Summary

Number Bet	Return on $1 Bet	Odds Paid	House Advantage
2	$30	29 to 1	16.6%
3	$15	14 to 1	16.6%
7	$5	4 to 1	16.6%
11	$15	14 to 1	16.6%
12	$30	29 to 1	16.6%
Any craps	$8	7 to 1	11.1%

As can be seen in the table, due to the excessively high house advantage, numbers bets are all very poor bets. Also note that the information on craps tables is misleading. "8 for 1" that is being offered for any craps does not mean that odds of 8 to 1 is being offered. It means that $8 will be returned for each $1 that has been bet. Since the $8 includes the $1 that was bet, the bet will actually be paid off at odds of 7 to 1.

Other One-Roll Bets

In addition to the field bet and the numbers bet, there are other infrequently used one-roll bets. Unfortunately, like the field bet and the numbers bet, the house advantage on these bets is high.

The "craps-eleven bet," which is more commonly referred to as the C-E bet, is a bet that a 2, 3, 11, or 12 will appear on the next roll. The craps (2, 3, or 12) pays 3 to 1. The 11 pays 7 to 1. To make this bet, give your chips to the stickman, who will place the chips in one of the small circles that are marked C and E at the center of the table.

A "hop bet" is a bet that the combination you have specified will appear on the next roll of the dice. You may specify any of the thirty-six possible combinations of the dice that might appear. For example, you might specify "5-3," "6-2" or "hardway 8." Since there is no way to distinguish between the two die, it should be noted that there are two possible combinations of a 5 and a 3, but only one possible combination of 4 and 4. Therefore, the payouts will be different. On any unpaired combination, the payout is 14 to 1 ($15 back on a $1 bet). For a paired combination, the payout is $29 to $1. There is no designated place on the table for a hop bet. Merely give your wager to the stickman and tell him how you would like to bet.

The "horn bet" is a bet that a 2, 3, 11, or 12 will appear on the next roll of the dice. Basically, this is a combined numbers bet on each of the four numbers. This bet must therefore be made on a multiple of four times the minimum table bet. If the 2 or 12 appears, you will get back $27 or each $4 that was bet, and if the 3 or 11 appears, you will get back $12. In essence, you will be paid for winning one bet with a deduction being made for three losing bets. Like the hop bet, there is no specified place for the horn bet on the craps table. Merely give your wager to the stickman and tell him that you wish to make a horn bet.

Craps California Style

In accordance with the Indian Gaming Regulatory Act of 1988, gaming in Indian casinos must comply with applicable state laws. Because gambling games that utilize dice are prohibited in the state of California, in some California casinos, you will see strange sights—craps games in which there are no dice. Instead of dice, the game is played with multiple decks of cards with seven through King deleted.

The cards are kept in two shoes, one shoe on each side of the dealer. Each shoe contains up to twenty decks of cards, with the cards in each shoe of a different color. One card is extracted from each shoe in order to determine the point for that "roll." Otherwise, on the surface, the game appears to be much the same as a regular craps game. However, outward appearances can be very deceiving. When played with dice, each roll is totally independent of all previous rolls. However, when played with cards, the cards that can be expected to appear out of the shoe will obviously depend on the cards that were in the shoe at the time the card was extracted from the shoe. Since a shoe that contains a disproportionately large number of big cards is more likely to produce a big point than a balanced deck and vice versa, if the deck contains a disproportionately large number of small cards, there may be possibilities here for a card counter.

Roulette Table Layout

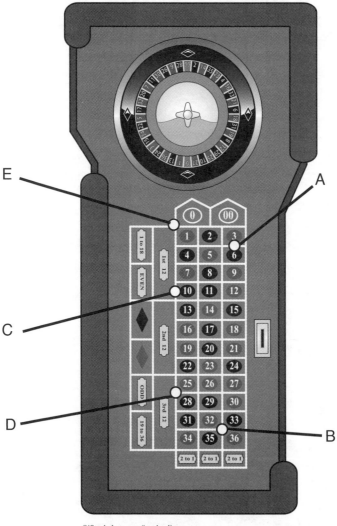

5. Roulette

Like baccarat, roulette is a game that was imported from the casinos of Europe. The American version of the game centers around a huge rotating wheel with thirty-eight slots that is set up beside an elaborate betting table. The slots are numbered 0, 00, and 1 through 36. The odd numbered slots are red, the even numbered slots are black, and the 0 and 00 are green. Although at first glance, the numbers might appear to be randomly placed, there is order. The 0 and 00 slots are directly opposite each other, each odd numbered slot is between two even numbers and is directly opposite its subsequent even number. Also, the small numbers and the large numbers are evenly dispersed around the wheel. With one exception, which is noted below, all bets at an American-style roulette table come with a rather high 5.26% house advantage. However, the mesmerizing effect of the colorful spinning wheel with the steel ball bouncing around inside and the high 35 to 1 payoff on the basic single number bet contributes to the continuing popularity of the roulette table in American casinos.

The roulette wheel is kept spinning at a moderate rate until the next game is about to begin. It then picks up speed and a small steel ball is released into the wheel in the opposite direction of the spin. As the wheel slows down, the betting is closed, and the ball drops into one of the thirty-eight slots, thereby designating the winning number.

In order to avoid confusion, each player at a roulette table is issued distinctly colored chips. The player determines the value of each chip at the time of purchase from one of the attendants.

However, the value is subject to some common sense limitations. For example, you will not be allowed to establish a value of $1 on a chip if the minimum bet at the table is $5. Chips from a roulette table cannot be used elsewhere in the casino and may not be taken from the table. There are two basic types of bets that may be made at a roulette table—inside bets and outside bets.

Inside Bets

A "Straight Bet," which is also known as a one-number bet, is made by placing a chip on the desired number. If the ball drops into the slot for the number that you have selected, the house will pay 35 to 1 on true odds of 37 to 1. You will therefore receive $36 back on a $1 bet.

A "Split Bet" is made by placing your chip on the line that separates two numbers (position A in the figure on page 62). If the ball settles in either numbered slot, the house will pay 17 to 1 ($18 back on each $1 that was bet).

A "Corner Bet" is made by placing your chip at the intersection of four numbered boxes (position B in the figure on page 62). If the ball settles in one of the four numbered slots, you will be paid at 8 to 1 ($9 back).

A "Street Bet" is made by placing a chip at the end of a three number row (position C in the figure on page 62). If the ball settles in one of the three slots, the house will pay off at 11 to 1.

A "Double Street Bet" is made by placing your bet on the line between two streets (position D in the figure on page 62) if the ball settles into one of the six slots, the house will pay at 5 to 1.

A "Five Number Bet" is made by placing your chip in the upper left corner of the box for the number one (position E in the figure on page 62). This is a bet that the ball will settle in the slot for 0, 00, 1, 2, or 3. If it does, the house will pay 6 to 1 ($7 back on a $1 bet). Since the house will have a 7.89% house advantage on this bet, this is the worst bet that you can make at a roulette table.

Outside Bets

Outside bets are bets that are made outside the numbered portion of the betting table. The following outside bets pay even money on odds of 20 to 18 (10 to 9).

"Red Bets" and "Black Bets" are made by placing chips in the box that indicates the color that was selected.

"Even Bets" and "Odd Bets" are made by placing chips in the box that indicates "even" or "odd."

"1 to 18 Bets" and "19 to 36 Bets" are made by placing chips in the appropriately marked boxes on the table.

The following outside bets pay 2 to 1 on odds of 26 to 12 (13 to 6).

A "Dozens Bet" is a bet on either the first, the second, or the third dozen numbers in the one through thirty-six sequentially numbered boxes on the betting table. These bets are made by placing chips in the boxes marked "1st 12," "2nd 12," or "3rd 12," as appropriate.

A "Column Bet" is a bet that the ball will fall into one of the three long, horizontal columns on the betting table. This bet is made by placing chips in the appropriate box that is marked "2 to 1" to the right of each column. Note that "0" and "00" are not included in any of the three columns. In fact, these two slots are included only in the somewhat artificially contrived five-number bet, which gives the house the largest house advantage at the table. The reason that these two slots are not included in any of the other combination bets is that they are the basis for the 5.26% house advantage.

With a thirty-eight slot wheel, American-style roulette is a relentlessly negative expectation game. Assuming that you never make a five-number bet, in the long run, you can expect to lose 5.26% of the total amount that you bet at the table. Therefore, if you make one hundred $10 bets, on average, you should expect to lose $52.60. Regardless of how much money you take with you into the casino, the law of averages and the 5.26% house advantage will eventually grind you into the ground. So what to do? Unless you are an expert poker player who thinks that you might be good enough to have a chance against the big boys in the poker room, read the appropriate chapter in this book and go over to a baccarat, blackjack, or craps table in which the house advantage is much lower. If you play wisely, at one of these tables, you should have a realistic shot at having a winning session. Otherwise, unless you have set aside a substantial bankroll for this session, do not linger too long at a roulette table. However, if you should get lucky, roulette is one of those games where it is truly wise to quit while you are still ahead.

Another alternative is to find a casino that uses a European-style roulette wheel that has only thirty-seven slots. With the 00 slot eliminated, the house advantage declines from 5.26% to 2.63%. Unfortunately, with the exception of a few casinos in Atlantic City, where high-limit roulette is played, there are few American casinos that use the European-style wheel. There is one other advantage of playing roulette in Atlantic City. If you make an even-money outside bet and the ball settles in either of the 0 or 00 slots, state gaming regulations allow the casino to take only one half of the amount that you had wagered. Even with the American-style wheel, this reduces the house advantage on even money bets to 2.63%.

Part II

Poker-Themed Table Games

Caribbean Stud

Let It Ride

Pai Gow Poker

Three Card Poker

The Rank and Frequency of Five-card Poker Hands

The games in this section are derived from poker and the payouts depend on the ranking of poker hands. The rank (strength) of a poker hand is based on the frequency with which that hand will appear when randomly dealt from a standard 52-card deck. For the 2,598,960 possible five-card hands this frequency is shown below.

Kind of Hand	Definition	Number Possible	Example
Royal Flush	Ace, King, Queen, Jack, 10, of the same suit.	4	A♦ K♦ Q♦ J♦ 10♦
Straight Flush	Five lesser sequential cards of the same suit.	36	9♣ 8♣ 7♣ 6♣ 5♣
Four of a Kind	Four cards of the same rank.	624	5♣ 5♦ 5♥ 5♠ 9♣
Full House	Three cards of one rank, two of another rank.	3744	8♣ 8♦ 8♠ J♥ J♣
Flush	Five cards of the same suit, not in sequence.	5108	A♠ J♠ 7♠ 3♠ 2♠
Straight	Five sequential cards, not of the same suit.	10,200	J♦ 10♠ 9♣ 8♦ 7♥
Three of a Kind	Three cards of the same rank, other two cards not paired.	54,912	6♦ 6♠ 6♣ 10♥ 2♣
Two Pair	Two cards of the same rank, two of another rank.	123,552	4♠ 4♣ 2♥ 2♣ 9♠
One Pair	Two cards of the same rank, other cards of various ranks.	1,098,240	9♣ 9♥ A♦ 10♦ 2♠
No Pair	No two cards of the same rank, cards not in sequence or of the same suit.	1,302,540	K♥ 10♠ 9♠ 6♥ 4♣

Caribbean Stud Table Layout

Dealer

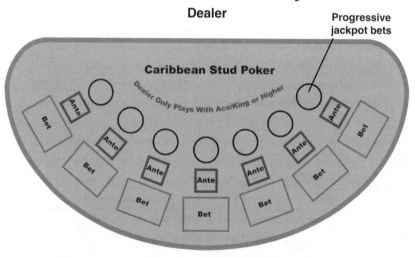

Progressive
jackpot bets

Players

6. Caribbean Stud

Caribbean Stud is a game that was first introduced to American casino gamblers aboard cruise ships that plied the Caribbean Sea. Like its close cousin "Let It Ride," it is a variation of Five-Card Stud poker. However, in Caribbean Stud, players are not merely trying to qualify for a payout based on an established payout schedule; they are also trying to beat the dealer's hand. The game is played on a small table similar to that which is shown in the figure.

The game begins with players placing the amount of their wagers in the Ante Boxes. Usually, the minimum bet will be $5. Players may also make side bets by placing $1 in the circle that is located above the Ante Box. This side bet, which is usually limited to a $1 bet, will be discussed later on.

After the dealer has accounted for the side bet, using a standard 52-card deck, she will deal each player, as well as herself, five cards face-down. She will then expose one of her cards. At this point, based on the qualifying hand table that follows, players must decide if their hand is strong enough to beat the dealer's hand.

Caribbean Stud Qualifying Hands

Hand	Description
Royal Flush	A, K, Q, J, and 10, in the same suit.
Straight Flush	Five cards in sequence, all in the same suit.
Four of a Kind	Four cards of the same rank.
Full House	Three cards of one rank, two cards also of equal rank.

Flush	Five cards in the same suit, not in sequence.
Straight	Five cards in sequence, not in the same suit.
Three of a Kind	Three cards of the same rank.
Two Pair	Two cards of one rank, two matched cards of another rank.
One Pair	Two cards of the same rank. Other cards of various ranks.
Ace-King High	No pairs, but the hand contains an Ace and a King.

If the player considers his hand to be strong enough to beat the dealer, he will call by placing double the amount of his ante into the Bet Box. If the player does not wish to call, he will fold by placing his cards face-down in front of him. The dealer will then pick up the cards in addition to the player's ante. After each player has acted on his hand in accordance with the foregoing, the dealer will then turn over her four remaining cards and determine if she has a qualifying hand as indicated in the previous table.

If the dealer does not have a qualifying hand, all remaining players win an amount equal to the ante, but do not receive payment on their call bet. The amount that was in the Bet Box is merely returned to the player.

If the dealer does have a qualifying hand, but the player still wins, the player will win even money on his ante and a bonus payment on his call bet as shown below.

Caribbean Stud Bonus Payout Table

Hand	Bonus
Royal Flush	100 to 1
Straight Flush	50 to 1
Four of a Kind	20 to 1
Full House	7 to 1
Flush	5 to 1
Straight	4 to 1
Three of a Kind	3 to 1
Two Pair	2 to 1
One Pair	1 to 1

If the dealer has the winning hand, the player will lose his ante as well as the amount that was in the Bet Box.

With a 52-card deck, a total of 2,598,960 different combinations of five cards are possible. Forty-four percent of these hands will not be qualifying hands. This means that, assuming that no player will call with a hand that does not even qualify, forty-four percent of the time that a player calls, he will have the dealer beat, but will not get paid for his call bet. In other words, if a player has a royal flush, which is an extreme 649,740 to 1 long shot (see the next chapter), there is a forty-four percent chance that he still will not win the meager 100 to 1 payout that is indicated in the Payout Table. If you have a low tolerance for frustrations of this type, a Caribbean Stud table is probably not the place for you, notwithstanding the fact that there are other tables in the casino that have a higher house advantage. Perhaps Let It Ride, which is discussed in the next chapter, might be better suited to your temperament.

Basic Playing Strategy

It is recommended that the call be made under the following circumstances:

- Whenever you have a pair (even a pair of deuces) in your hand. This recommendation is based on the fact that if you do not make the call, you will forfeit your ante and there is a 50% chance that the dealer will not even have a pair in his hand. Do not be intimidated if the dealer is showing a "scare" card such as an Ace or a King. If you have a pair of deuces, you would prefer that the dealer show an Ace or King rather than a three. Why? Because if an Ace or King helps the dealer make a qualifying hand, it will probably be an Ace-King high hand which your lowly pair of deuces will beat, thereby qualifying you for a bonus payment. However, it makes no difference to you whether you lose to a pair of Aces or a pair of threes.

• Whenever you do not have a pair, but do have an Ace and King as high cards. However, exercise caution if the dealer is showing an Ace or King because your third highest card then becomes very important. If the dealer is showing an Ace or King, call only if your third highest card is a queen.

The Progressive Jackpot

One way to avoid frustrations of the type that were described in the previous paragraph is to participate in the progressive jackpot. However, the cost may be high. Payouts from the progressive jackpot are totally independent of the basic game. In other words, payment will be made without regard to whether or not the dealer has a qualifying hand. A typical payout table for the progressive jackpot is shown below. However, there may be significant differences between casinos.

Caribbean Stud Progressive Jackpot Table

Hand	Payout
Royal Flush	100% of jackpot
Straight Flush	50% of jackpot
Four of a Kind	$100
Full House	$ 75
Flush	$ 50

The size of the jackpot depends on the amount that was collected from previous progressive jackpot participants. In general, immediately after the jackpot has been hit, the casino will "seed" the new jackpot for a predetermined amount. Thereafter, a percentage of each progressive jackpot collection will go towards increasing the jackpot until it is again hit.

Note that the odds of getting a royal flush with five random cards are almost 650,000 to 1. To put this into perspective, if you were to play 50 hands per hour, 40 hours per week, 52 weeks each year, with average luck, you should expect to get a royal flush approximately once every 6.25 years. Giving consideration to the fact that during that time, you will have many thousands of other smaller winning hands, it is estimated that participation in a progressive jackpot pool, as is described above, will not have a positive expectation unless the jackpot is more than $200,000. However, this may vary greatly between casinos because some casinos pay different amounts for flushes, full houses and four of a kind than is shown in the table on page 74. Some casinos also make payments for straights. Regardless, because payment from this progressive jackpot pool is made only for a few long shot hands, participation in this pool should be expected to result in a substantial drain on your funds, unless of course, you happen to get extremely lucky and hit the big one.

Let It Ride Table Layout

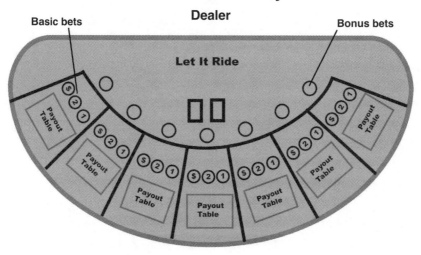

Players

7. Let It Ride

Let It Ride is a game that was developed by Shuffle Masters, Incorporated, a manufacturer of card shuffling machines. Reportedly, it was created in order to help spur sales of Shuffle Master machines. The game is a rather ingenious variation of Five-Card Stud and is played on a small table similar to that which is shown in the figure.

The game begins with the player placing bets in the small circles marked $, 2, and 1. An equal amount must be wagered in each circle. The dealer will then activate the card shuffling machine which will emit seven groups of cards with three cards in each group. The cards will then be distributed to each position, including positions that are not occupied. The last group will go to the dealer who will place the top card in the box to the dealer's right and the second card in the box to the dealer's left. The last card, along with the balance of the deck will be discarded. The last two cards remaining in front of the dealer, along with the three cards that were distributed to each player, will constitute the player's five-card poker hand.

Unlike in a regular poker game, players at a Let it Ride table are not competing against other players at the table, but are merely trying to qualify for a payout. Because this is a proprietary game, the payouts are largely standard. A typical payout schedule, which is also shown on actual playing tables, is shown next. For illustrative purposes, I have also shown the frequency with which these hands can be expected to appear in a randomly dealt five-card poker hand.

Let It Ride Payout Table

Qualifying Hand	Payout	Frequency
Royal Flush	1,000 to 1	1 in 649,739 hands
Straight Flush	200 to 1	1 in 72,192 hands
Four of a Kind	50 to 1	1 in 4,164 hands
Full House	11 to 1	1 in 693 hands
Flush	8 to 1	1 in 508 hands
Straight	5 to 1	1 in 254 hands
Three of Kind	3 to 1	1 in 46 hands
Two Pair	2 to 1	1 in 20 hands
Pair: Tens or higher	1 to 1	1 in 5 hands

Lest a comparison of the Payout and Frequency columns instill unjustified negativity about the game, it should be pointed out that although the true odds against receiving a royal flush with five random cards are 649,730 to one, there are many lesser payouts, and players may withdraw two-thirds of their original bets if the first three cards are not promising. For example, if you had bet $5 in each of the three circles mentioned above and your first three cards included a pair of Jacks, you will be guaranteed a $15 win on the $15 total that you had placed in the three circles. In addition, if the two cards that the dealer will expose turns out to be Jacks, you will win a total of $750 (50 x $5 x 3). With enlightened play, it is estimated that the house advantage on this game is approximately 3.5%, which is not exorbitant when compared to many other games in the casino. In fact, many casino patrons prefer this game to baccarat, which has a lower house advantage, because Let It Ride offers the potential for a relatively large payout, while actually risking only a small amount. The fact that Let It Ride offers the patron a greater role in actually "playing" the game adds to the game's appeal.

After the dealer has discarded the excess cards, each player, in turn, will be offered the option to withdraw the amount in the number 1 circle or "let it ride." If you wish to withdraw the bet, simply scratch the table with the cards that are in your hands.

The dealer will then push the chips that are in the circle back to you. If you want to "let it ride," place your cards under the chips that are in circle 1 and the dealer will proceed to the next player.

After all players have exercised this first option, the dealer will expose the community card on her left and the same procedure will be repeated. The option to withdraw the chips in circle 2 is completely independent of the first option. In other words, whether you removed your chips from the circle or "let it ride," you will still have the option to remove the chips from circle 2 or again "let it ride."

After all players have exercised the second option, the dealer will turn over each player's cards and make settlement in accordance with the payout table.

Basic Playing Strategy

Once a player has decided on the amount that he will wager, his only strategy consideration is the decision to withdraw a portion of his wager. Actually, the option to withdraw a portion of his original wager or "let it ride" is nothing more than a rather clever marketing ploy because the fact that a player is permitted to withdraw up to two-thirds of his bet if the prospects do not appear to be promising is the most appealing aspect of the game. In fact, it would probably lead to wiser decision making if players thought of the amount in the $ circle as the amount of the bet and each option as an opportunity to make an additional bet. The reason is that some players, especially among younger males, consider it macho to "let it ride" even when the prospects would not justify an additional bet. However, nobody would consider it macho to put fresh money on the table in order to make a dumb bet.

For any moderately knowledgeable poker player, the second option (after seeing four cards) is a relatively simple one because the odds of making a payout-qualifying hand can be readily calculated and the payout is shown on the table. For example, if your four cards are 7♦, 8♦, 9♦, 9♣, it would not be wise to "let it ride." The reason is that, not counting the four cards that you can see, there are forty-eight cards remaining in the deck. Of these forty-eight cards, only eight (7♥, 7♣, 7♠, 8♥, 8♣, 8♠, 9♥, and 9♠) will give you a payout-qualifying hand. This means that your chances of making a payout-qualifying hand are only 1 in 6 (8/48=1/6), but the best possible payout is only 3 to 1 for three 9s.

Applying this same principle, four cards to a small or medium straight, such as 5♦, 6♦, 7♦, 8♣, is not playable because there are only eight cards (the four 4s and the four 9s) that will complete the straight. Therefore, you can expect to complete only one-sixth of these hands. However, a straight pays only 5 to 1.

Very different is the high straight draw such as 10♦, J♦, Q♦, K♣. In addition to the eight cards that will complete the straight, twelve cards will pair one of the four cards that you are holding and qualify you for a 1 to 1 payout. This is, therefore, an excellent drawing hand.

The decision on the second option is a relatively straightforward decision based on the payout table and the probability of making a hand that will qualify for a payout. Somewhat more complex is the decision on the first option, which must be based on a two-stage probability. Consider a starting hand such as 5♦, 6♦, 8♦. If a 7♦ is the first common card that the dealer exposes, the player will have an open-ended draw to a straight flush, which will pay out at odds of 200 to 1. However, there is only one chance in forty-nine that the 7♦ will appear. The 4♦ and 9♦ will give the player an inside straight flush-draw but there are only two chances that either of those two cards will appear. In short, it is a long shot that the first common card will leave open the possibility of making a straight flush. If the possibility does materialize, it is still another long shot that the straight flush will be made. Notwithstanding the fact that you are in the casino to gamble and there is also the possibility of making a flush which will pay 8 to 1, it would be a questionable decision to "let it ride" on this first option; especially since if the straight flush possibility does develop, you will still have an opportunity to "let it ride" on your second option and have a chance to cash in at 200 to 1 on two bets.

Option Strategy

Based on the payout table and mathematical probability, it is recommended that you "let it ride" in the following instances.

First Option

- Your first three cards already qualify for a payout.
- Your first three cards consist of three consecutive cards of the same suit and your smallest card is at least a 3. Examples: 3♦, 4♦, 5♦ and 10♣, J♣, Q♣.
- Your first three cards (1) have the potential to become a straight flush (2) at least one of your cards is higher than a nine and (3) there is no more than one gap between your three cards. Examples: 8♦, 9♦, J♦ and 7♣, 8♣, 10♣.
- Your first three cards have the potential to become a straight flush with at least two cards higher than a 9. Examples: 8♦, 10♦, Q♦ and 8♣, 10♣, Q♣.

Second option

- Your first four cards already qualify for a payout.
- Your first four cards are all the same suit.
- Your first four cards are not the same suit, but they are consecutive and the largest card is at least a Jack.

Bonus Payments

In addition to the three basic bets that have been discussed earlier, players have an option to make a bonus side bet for $1. The payout table for this special bonus side bet usually varies between casinos and typically appears to be far more generous than the basic payout table that was shown earlier in this chapter. Typically, the top payout for this special bonus table is $20,000 for a royal flush, which can be very enticing to the novice for a $1 bet. However, a royal flush is a 649,739 to 1 long shot.

When consideration is given to the fact that two-thirds of your basic bet can be withdrawn but no part of the bonus side bet can be withdrawn, it becomes obvious that this bonus side bet is no bargain. It is a typical "get rich quick" sucker bet. Over the course of a night, those bucks will add up very rapidly.

Some casinos have recently added a new wrinkle to the game: a three-card bonus option. For this option, payment is made for qualifying hands that are contained in the player's initial three cards. Qualifying hands and amounts that will be paid vary between casinos. In essence, an element of Three Card Poker, a game that is discussed in Chapter 9, has been added to Let It Ride.

Cautionary Closing Note

Most casinos have a limit on the amount that will be paid out on any given hand. This could be as little as $25,000. Therefore, if you bet $25 in each circle and make a royal flush, you might not receive the expected $75,000. In order to avoid any possible misunderstanding, check this out before sitting down at a table.

Pai Gow Poker Table Layout

Dealer

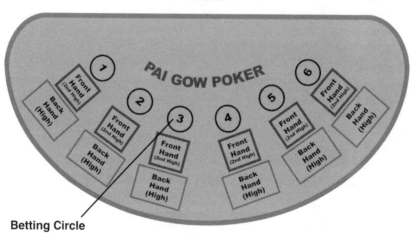

Betting Circle

Players

8. Pai Gow Poker

Pai gow poker is a concoction of American-style poker and an ancient Chinese gambling game that was played with small black tiles upon which Chinese characters had been inscribed. The game was introduced to American casino patrons in the cardrooms of California twenty short years ago, but quickly mushroomed across the country.

Pai gow poker is played with a 53-card deck that includes a Joker. In the vast majority of casinos, the Joker may be used only as an Ace or as any card that will complete a straight, a flush or a straight flush. However, in a few casinos, the Joker may be used as any card that will maximize the strength of the hand. This means that, like in some home poker games, the Joker is a true "wild" card. Since in the vast majority of casinos, the Joker can be used only as an Ace or as part of a straight or flush, comments and recommendations contained herein are applicable only to such games.

Unlike in an American-style poker game, players are not playing against other players at the table but against a banker. The banker is usually a house dealer. However, because California law prohibits casinos from banking card games, in California cardrooms one of the players serves as the banker. In order to qualify as the banker, however, a player must commit a sufficient amount of money to cover the anticipated wagers of all other players at the table. A few casinos outside of California also permit players to serve as bankers.

As a fee for playing, the casino (a) deducts five percent from each winning bet or (b) collects a fixed amount from each winning bet. In most cases, the five percent charge is preferable for the small stakes player and the fixed fee is more desirable for the high roller. This writer has seen pai gow poker games in which a minimum $1 fee is charged for each bet that is made up to $100. For bets in excess of $100, an additional $1 is charged for each fraction of $100. This means that the casino will be taking 10% of the winnings on a $10 bet, which borders on the usurious.

Pai gow poker is played on a small table similar to that which is shown in the figure on page 84. After bets have been made by placing chips in the betting circles, the dealer will deal out seven hands face-down consisting of seven cards each. After insuring that there are four cards remaining in her hand, the dealer will discard the four cards and turn her attention to a small tea-cup-like device that holds three dice, which she will hand to one of the players. After shaking the cup vigorously, that player will set the cup on the table. The dealer will then lift the cup, thereby revealing the three dice. The total of the three dice determines which player will receive the first hand. For this purpose, the banker's position is designated as position number 1. Since there are seven positions at the table and the three dice may total as much as eighteen, the banker's number is also designated as 8 and 15. If the total of the dice is 6, the dealer will count counterclockwise starting with the banker's position as number 1 and count to 6. This means that in games in which the dealer also serves as the banker, the first hand will go to seat #5 in the diagram of the table. If the total of the dice is 11, the first hand will go to seat #3.

After determining which position should receive the first hand, the dealer will then continue clockwise in distributing the six remaining hands. Any hand that might have gone to a seat that is not occupied will be discarded. Therefore, the number of players that are at the table will have no bearing on the hand that a player would have received. In fact, the practice of using dice to determine which hand will go to each player has no impact on a player's chances because although the dice do randomly determine which hand you will receive, since the cards themselves were randomly dealt, the dice have no impact on a player's chances. The procedure does, however, seem to add a sense of intrigue and charm to the game. Unfortunately, many casinos no longer use the teacup and dice. Instead, in order to speed up play and increase profits, an automatic shuffling machine spits out the hands and a random number generator determines which cards will go to the various seats.

The object of pai gow poker is to create two poker hands, one hand consisting of two cards and another consisting of five cards that can beat the two hands that the banker will create. The strongest possible two-card hand, which we will refer to as the front hand, is a pair of Aces. The strongest possible five-card hand, which we will refer to as the "back hand," is five Aces. For the back hand, the normal ranking of hands that apply to American-style poker are applicable. The ranking of poker hands, following the addition of five Aces, is the same as normal five-card poker with the exception that a hand of five Aces, out ranks all other hands, including a royal flush.

In every case, the hands must be set so that the back hand will be equal to or stronger than the front hand. If this is not done, the hand is fouled and the bet is lost.

Players (other than any player who might be acting as the banker) will set their hands by placing two cards (the front hand) in the horizontal box on the table. The remaining five cards, which will constitute the back hand, will be placed in the vertical box. After all players have completed setting their hand, the dealer will turn over the banker's cards and set the hand in the "house way." The house way is the way that is considered to be the most advantageous to the banker. However, if one of the players is serving as the banker, that player will have the option of rearranging the cards, provided that the back hand is at least as strong as the front hand. Incidentally, any player who wishes to have his hand set in the house way may have the dealer do so by simply pushing his cards to the dealer before the dealer exposes the banker's cards. Like the banker, such players are also free to make changes after seeing what the dealer has recommended.

After the banker's hand has been set, the dealer will expose each player's hand in turn and compare it with the banker's hand. First, the player's front hand will be compared to the banker's front hand. Then the back hands will be compared. If the hands that are being compared are of equal strength, the hands are said to be "copies." The banker wins all copies, which gives a player who is serving as the banker an advantage of approximately 1.25% over other players at the table. Obviously, it is wise to serve as the banker whenever possible.

Setting Your Hand

In order for a player to win his bet, the player's front hand must beat the dealer's front hand and the player's back hand must beat the banker's back hand in head-to-head match-ups. If the player wins one of the match-ups but loses or ties in the other match-up, the bet is a push. If the player loses both match-ups or loses one match-up and ties in the other match-up, the player loses his bet. With this in mind, the following guidance is provided relative to setting hands in pai gow poker.

How to Set Pai Gow Hands

Cards in Front Hand	Cards in Back Hand
Hands Containing No Pairs, Straights or Flushes	
Second and third highest cards	Highest card
Hands With One Pair	
Two highest unpaired cards	Pair
Hands With Two Pairs (Including a Pair of Aces)	
Small pair	Pair of Aces
Hands With Two Large Pairs (Both Larger Than 8's)	
Smaller pair	Larger pair

Cards in Front Hand   **Cards in Back Hand**

Hands With Two Small Pairs, (Both Smaller Than 6's)

Small pair   Bigger pair

As an exception, if you have an Ace and/or an unpaired King that you can put in the front hand, keep both pairs together in the back hand.

Other Hands That Include Two Pairs

Small pair   Bigger pair

This applies to hands containing two pair that do not fit into one of the three categories listed above. As an exception, if you have an unpaired Ace that you can put in the front hand *and* the smaller of your pairs consists of deuces or threes, keep both pairs together in the back hand.

Hands Containing Three Pairs

Largest pair   Two smaller pair

Hands Containing Three of a Kind, Other than Aces

Two highest unpaired cards   Three of a kind

Hands Containing Three Aces

One of the Aces   Pair of Aces

As an exception, if your hand includes a King and one other face card, keep the three Aces together in the back hand and put the King and a face card in the front hand.

Hands Containing Two Sets*

Pair from large set   Small set

---

* A "set" means three of a kind.

Cards in Front Hand   **Cards in Back Hand**

Hands Containing a Straight or a Flush and Two Pairs

Ignore straight or flush and play as a hand with two pairs.

Other Straights and Flushes

Keep a straight or flush for the back hand. However, put the two highest possible cards in the front hand, even if that will weaken the straight or flush.

Hands Containing a Full House

Pair   Three of a kind

Hands Containing Four 2s, 3s, 4s, 5s, and 6s

Two largest unpaired cards.   Four of a kind

Hands Containing Four 7s, 8s 9s, l0s, and Jacks

Put a pair in both the front and back hands unless you have an Ace that you can put in the front hand. In such case, put four of a kind in the back hand.

Hands Containing Four Queens, Kings or Aces

Put a pair in both the front and back hands.

Straight and Royal Flushes

Play as you would any other straight or flush.

As was indicated earlier, casinos all have a house way that will be used by their pai gow dealers when deciding how to set their hand. Although for the most part, the house way will generally closely follow the guidelines that have been provided above, there may be slight differences between casinos on how a dealer will play some hands, particularly those hands that contain two pairs. The reason is that, with the millions of seven-card pai gow poker hands that can be dealt from a 53-card deck, the mathematics of properly playing every single hand can become impossibly complex. Therefore, in the interest of simplicity, most of the casinos have developed their own house way that will be easy for their dealers to remember, yet result in uniformity and generally sound play throughout the casino.

Casinos make available to their patrons a small index card or flyer that will explain their house way. If you are not familiar with the house way, ask for a copy because it may provide you with some very useful information. For example, in many casinos, if the dealer has two pairs that are smaller than 6s, the two pairs will always be placed in the back hand, regardless of what the three unpaired cards may be. If you are playing in such a casino and you have two pairs consisting of 7s and 4s, as an exception to the guidelines shown above, it would be wise to keep the two pairs for the back hand if you have an Ace that you could play in the front hand. The reason is that your two small pairs in the back hand will be extremely strong because any two pairs that the dealer will have in the back hand will very likely be two smaller pairs. If the dealer did have two pairs that would have beaten your 7s and 4s, the probability is very high that she would have split them between the front and back hands.

The message here is that the house dealer must set her hand in a manner that is consistent with the house way, but you do not have to. I therefore suggest that you be flexible, bearing in mind that your objective is to win the bet. However, if you do not think that you can possibly win the bet, try to get a push. Keep in mind that an Ace and a King in the front hand is not significantly weaker than a very small pair. However, if you put the second pair in the back hand, it will greatly strengthen the back hand.

Three Card Poker Table Layout

Dealer

Players

The Rank and Frequency of Three-Card Poker Hands

Just as for five-card poker, the rank (strength) of a three-card poker hand is based on the frequency with which that hand will appear when randomly dealt from a standard 52-card deck. For Three Card Poker there are 22,100 possible hands. The frequencies of the hands are shown in the table below. Note that compared to five-card poker, the hand rankings are very different when only three cards are dealt.

Kind of Hand	Definition	Number Possible	Example
Straight Flush	Three sequential cards of the same suit.	48	8♣ 7♣ 6♣
Three of a Kind	Three cards of the same rank.	52	5♣ 5♦ 5♥
Straight	Three sequential cards, not of the same suit.	720	J♥ 10♠ 9♣
Flush	Three cards of the same suit, not in sequence.	1096	J♠ 7♠ 2♠
One Pair	Two cards of the same rank, one card of another rank.	3744	9♣ 9♥ A♦
No Pair	No two cards of the same rank, cards not in sequence or of the same suit.	16,440	K♥ 10♠ 4♣

9. Three Card Poker

Three Card Poker is the latest and the simplest poker-derived table game to debut in American casinos. The game is played on a small table that closely resembles a Caribbean Stud table. The only significant difference is that the three betting boxes are labeled Ante, Play, and Pair Plus. In a sense, the game is two totally independent games that can be played simultaneously. These two games, which are generally referred to as Pair Plus and Beat the Dealer, will be discussed separately.

Pair Plus

By placing a chip in the Pair Plus box, the player is betting that his three-card hand will include at least a pair. If his hand does not include at least a pair, the player will lose the amount in the Pair Plus box. If his hand does include at least a pair, the player receives payment based on the strength of his hand as indicated in the table.

Payout Table for Pair Plus

Hand	Description	Payout
Straight Flush	Three consecutive cards of the same suit	40 to 1
Three of a Kind	Three cards of same rank	30 to 1
Straight	Three cards in sequence, different suits	6 to 1
Flush	Three of the same suit, not in sequence	4 to 1
Pair	Two of the three cards are of the same rank	1 to 1

Note that the ranking of hands for Three Card Poker is very different than for a regular five-card game of poker. This is because in poker, the strength of a hand depends on the frequency with which a hand can be expected to appear. For this reason, in a five-card game of poker, a flush ranks higher than three of a kind. However, in Three Card Poker, a flush will appear with much greater frequency than three of a kind. (See the hand rankings on page 92.) Therefore, the payout table on page 93 indicates that three of a kind pays 30 to 1, but a flush pays only 4 to 1. Note also that a straight ranks higher than a flush and there is no royal flush. Actually, in five-card a royal flush is nothing more than the highest possible straight flush. Perhaps casino management realized that some big payments might be avoided by not making a special category for the highest-ranking straight flush.

Beat the Dealer

A player who wishes to play Beat the Dealer does so by placing a bet in the Ante Box. The amount need not be the same as the amount that may have been placed in the Pair Plus Box. Players are free to play Pair Plus, Beat the Dealer, or both games simultaneously.

After looking at your cards, you must decide if your hand is strong enough to beat the dealer's hand. If you think that you can beat the dealer, you must place an amount equal to your ante into the Play Box. If you are not confident that you can beat the dealer, you may fold by pushing your cards face-down to the dealer, who will pick up your cards and your ante.

After each player has acted on his hand, the dealer will turn her cards over. As in Caribbean Stud, the first step is to determine if she has a qualifying hand. All hands that are listed in the preceding table are qualifying hands. In addition, any other hand that includes at least an Ace, a King or a Queen is a qualifying hand. If the dealer does not have a qualifying hand, she will fold and make payment at the rate of $1 for every $1 in the Ante Box. She will refund, but will not make payment on any amount that was in the Play Box.

If the dealer does have a qualifying hand, each player's hand will be turned over and compared to the dealer's hand. If the dealer's hand ranks higher than the player's hand, the player will lose both his Ante and Play bets.

If the player's hand ranks higher than the dealer's hand, the player will be paid even money on both his Ante and Play bets. In addition, if the player has a straight, three of a kind, or straight flush, he will receive a bonus payment on the ante bet as indicated in the following table. This bonus payment will be made even if you cannot beat the dealer's hand.

Bonus Payout Table for Beat the Dealer

Hand	Payout
Straight Flush	5 to 1
Three of a Kind	4 to 1
Straight	1 to 1

Basic Playing Strategy

For Pair Plus, there really is no playing strategy, because once the bet has been made, the game automatically plays to conclusion. The house advantage on this bet is generally estimated to be approximately 2.3%, which is considered to be quite reasonable when compared to most other table games in the casino. However, a word of warning is appropriate. Playing rules, including payout rates, may vary considerably between various casinos. Most of the changes that you will find can be expected to result in an increase in the house advantage.

For Beat the Dealer, the correct strategy is to make the Play Bet whenever your hand is strong enough to have been a qualifying hand were it in the possession of the dealer. Otherwise, fold the hand. As was indicated previously, house rules for this game may vary considerably between casinos. However, in general, the house advantage for a Pair Plus bet is usually slightly more favorable (less unfavorable) to the player than the Beat the Dealer bet.

Part III

Machine-Based Games

Keno

Slot Machines

Video Poker

©iStockphoto.com/spxChrome

10. Keno

Keno is a game for the casual, laid back casino gambler because it can be played while dining, enjoying a drink in the cocktail lounge, or even swimming in the hotel pool. The game also has the advantage of accepting very small bets and offering some huge payoffs. Unfortunately, it also has the disadvantage of having some of the longest odds outside of the state lottery.

Although bets can be made through keno runners who circulate throughout the casino, the game itself is conducted in the keno lounge, which is usually set off from the rest of the casino by curtains or luxuriously padded walls. Unlike the rest of the casino which can sometimes get very noisy with clanging bells, ringing buzzers, and occasional shouts of joy, the mood in a keno lounge is usually subdued and tranquil. On the far wall of the lounge, you usually will find a huge electronic board containing boxes numbered from one to eighty. If a game has just been completed, twenty of the boxes will be lit. Just below the board, you can expect to find the ticket writer's desk where bets are accepted, and a very large display case containing what looks like numbered ping pong balls floating around inside. Circulating around among the lounge chairs, which have small arms that are useful for writing keno tickets, you usually will find a cocktail waitress taking orders for free drinks.

Depending on the time of day and the number of patrons in the casino, games are usually conducted in intervals of approximately ten minutes. After bets have been taken, the number-selecting machine randomly selects twenty numbered balls, and these numbers are lit up on the big board in the keno lounge, as well as on smaller boards that are situated throughout the casino. When the last of the twenty numbers has been selected, that number will flash on and off for several seconds in order to alert viewers to the fact that the number selection process has been completed. These boards will also indicate the game number for which the lighted numbers apply. It is extremely important to pay attention to the game number because in most casinos, a winning ticket must be redeemed before the next game begins. Tickets that are not redeemed on a timely basis are invalid, and excuses such as "I was in the ladies room" are not likely to get a sympathetic hearing because they have all been heard before. If you find this limitation to be burdensome, a solution might be a "Multiple-Game Ticket." A Multiple-Game Ticket permits a patron to play the same numbers for as many as a thousand consecutive games. It is also extremely important to treat winning tickets like cash because there is nothing on the ticket that can identify you as the owner of the ticket. Therefore, anybody can take your ticket to the cashier's cage and cash it in.

Like the state lotteries, the object of keno is to guess which numbers will be selected by the number-selecting machine. For this purpose, tickets that are similar to the figure on page 101 are made available throughout the casino.

In most casinos, you will be permitted to select anywhere from one to fifteen numbers. As is shown in the figure on the right, clearly mark an "X" over each number that you have selected using the crayon that will be supplied by the casino. The example shown in the figure indicates that 12 numbers have been selected and that $1 is being wagered on the ticket. The minimum amount that may be wagered on a ticket varies with the casino, but in some casinos may be less than one dollar.

Normally, a ticket is good for only one game. For information on such things as the number of spots that may be marked on a ticket, minimum and maximum bets allowed, amounts that will be paid. etc., obtain a copy of the keno information booklet at the ticket writer's desk.

Straight Keno Ticket

<table>
<tr><td colspan="2" align="center">**KENO TICKET**</td><td align="center">Total Bet
$1</td></tr>
</table>

1	2	✗	✗	5	6	7	8	9	10
11	12	✗	✗	✗	16	17	18	19	20
21	22	23	24	25	26	27	28	29	30
31	32	33	34	35	36	37	38	39	40

12

41	42	43	44	45	46	47	✗	✗	✗
51	52	53	54	55	56	57	58	59	60
61	62	63	64	✗	✗	67	68	69	70
71	72	73	74	75	76	77	78	✗	✗

In order to actually place your bet, take your ticket to the ticket writer's desk or give your ticket and money to a keno runner. As a receipt, you will be given a copy of an official ticket that will indicate the numbers that were selected, the date, the game number and the amount that was wagered. Be sure that you check your ticket for accuracy before the number selection process begins.

Keno payout schedules may vary considerably between casinos. However, the odds do not. It may therefore be wise to compare payout schedules before deciding where to play. Following is a table that indicates amounts that will be paid by the typical casino for a winning $1 ticket on which one, five, and twelve spots have been marked. Also shown on the table are the true odds. On this table, figures that are shown under the "Catch" column refer to the quantity of numbers that were marked on the ticket that were later selected by the number-selecting machine. In other words, these are the "correct" numbers that are on a ticket.

Keno Payouts Compared to Odds

Total Numbers Selected	Catch	Payout for $1 Bet	True Odds
1	1	$3	3 to 1
5	3	$1	11 to 1
5	4	$7	82 to 1
5	5	$850	1550 to 1
12	6	$5	30 to 1
12	7	$35	140 to 1
12	8	$200	980 to 1
12	9	$1600	10,500 to 1
12	10	$4000	184,000 to 1
12	11	$20,000	5,900,000 to 1
12	12	$50,000	471,000,000 to 1

Figures that are shown under the Payout column indicate amounts that you will receive back for a winning $1 bet. These amounts include the $1 that you originally had bet. Therefore, if you had selected only one number and the number-selecting machine did "catch" your number, you will actually be winning $2. In essence, the casino will be paying you at the rate of 2 to 1 on odds of 3 to 1. This amounts to a house advantage of 25%, which in a sense makes the one number bet the best bet that you will find in a keno lounge. When considering the fact that even on a high house advantage game such as roulette, the casino patron can make bets that will pay 2 to 1 with only a 5.26% house advantage, it becomes obvious that keno is not a game for those who are serious about winning money in a casino.

There is a further cautionary note. All casinos have limits on the aggregate amount that will be paid on a game. Therefore, if the aggregate amount is $50,000 and by some miracle, all twelve numbers on your $10 ticket appear on the board, you will not be paid $500,000 but a maximum of $50,000.

The figure on page 101 shows a ticket upon which twelve numbers have been marked. This is a ticket that is valid for only one game. As is indicated on the ticket, $1 is being wagered.

Such a ticket, which is known as a "straight ticket," is largely self-explanatory.

Split Keno Ticket

A blank keno ticket may be used to bet in numerous different ways. The next figure shows what is known as a "split ticket." A split ticket is a keno ticket on which more than one bet is made by splitting the numbers that are shown on the ticket into two or more separate bets. In essence, the numbers that have been shown on the ticket are "split" into more than one bet. In split ticket example, the twelve numbers that were marked in the first figure on page 101 are separated by a line into two groups, one consisting of five numbers and one consisting of seven numbers. This separation of the numbers may also be accomplished by circling both groups of numbers. After splitting the numbers into two groups, this ticket will serve as two separate straight tickets. The figures that are shown on the right side of the ticket indicate that one 5-number bet and one 7-number bet are being made, and that 50¢ is being wagered on

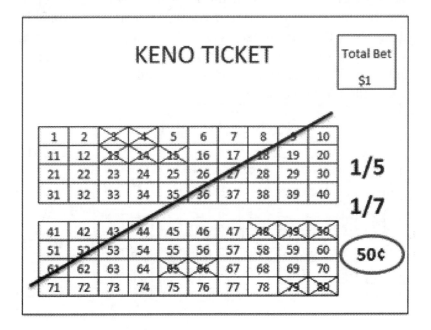

each of the two bets. In most casinos, the minimum that may be bet on each separate bet on a ticket on which two or more bets have been made is less than the minimum amount that will be required on a straight ticket. However, the total amount that is wagered on such a ticket must be at least as much as would be required on a straight ticket.

Way Keno Ticket

The most popular keno ticket is the "way ticket," which is a ticket on which the numbers that were marked are grouped into three or more groups, each consisting of an equal quantity of numbers as is shown in the figure below. These separate groups may then be combined in order to create what amounts to several straight tickets. The figure indicates that the six numbers that have been selected are being used to make three bets consisting of four numbers each and that 50¢ is being wagered on each bet. The four-number groupings are: 1-2-39-40, 1-2-79-80, and 39-40-79-80. Note how this is indicated on the right side of the keno ticket. The top half of the fraction indicates the number of "ways" that the numbers are being grouped. The bottom portion of the fraction indicates the quantity of numbers that are in each group. The amount that is being wagered on each "way" is then indicated below the fraction, and the total amount that is being wagered is indicated in the box at the top of the ticket.

Combination Way Keno Ticket

Another popular method of preparing a keno ticket is known as the "combination way ticket" shown in the next figure. This ticket differs from the basic way ticket in that it creates groups containing different quantities of numbers. In the figure below the following bets are being made:

- **Four six-number bets:** 1-2-39-40-49-50, 1-2-39-40-79-80, 1 -2-49-50-79-80, and 39-40-49-50-79-80.
- **Six four-number bets:** 1-2-39-40, 1-2-49-50, 1-2-79-80, 39-40-49-50, 39-40-79-80, 49-50-79-80.

Demonstrating the versatility of the combination way ticket, it should be noted that the following additional combination bets could have been made, using the same ticket that is shown below.

- **Four two-number bets:** 1-2, 39-40, 49-50, and 79-80.
- **One eight-number bet:** 1-2-39-40-49-50-79-80.

KENO TICKET

Total Bet
$ 3.50

✗	✗	3	4	5	6	7	8	9	10
11	12	13	14	15	16	17	18	19	20
21	22	23	24	25	26	27	28	29	30
31	32	33	34	35	36	37	38	✗	✗

4/6
50¢

41	42	43	44	45	46	47	48	✗	✗
51	52	53	54	55	56	57	58	59	60
61	62	63	64	65	66	67	68	69	70
71	72	73	74	75	76	77	78	✗	✗

6/4
25¢

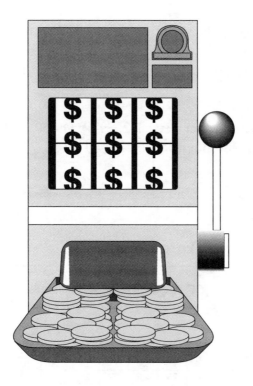

11. Slot Machines

For many years, the basic slot machine in American casinos was the one-armed bandit. These machines were rather crude mechanical devices that were activated by dropping a coin into a slot and then pulling down on a long steel arm that set three rollers in motion. When the rollers stopped, a symbol from each roller appeared in a narrow window on the machine. If the symbols matched a payout table that appeared on the machine, the machine noisily dropped the appropriate number of coins into a coin tray. Because each roller could accommodate only twenty symbols, there were only 8,000 possible combinations (20 x 20 x 20) that could appear in the window. Although modifications were later made in order to increase the number of symbols on each roller and the number of coins that could be inserted into the machine before pulling down on the steel arm, these mechanical slot machines were very limited in the maximum payout that could be offered.

From this humble beginning, slot machines have evolved into highly sophisticated computer-controlled electronic devices that dominate the casino scene to such an extent that two-thirds of the profit from the typical American casino now comes from slot machines. In the broadest sense, there are now two categories of slot machines. The direct descendent of the old mechanical slot machine is the computer-controlled electronic slot machine. Like the original slot machine, once activated, these machines automatically continue to the conclusion of play without further action of the slot player. These machines, which I refer to as electronic slot machines, or simply slot machines, will be discussed in this chapter.

A direct offshoot of the electronic slot machine is the video gaming machine. These are machines which, like the electronic slot machine, are activated by the push of a button, but require active participation of the slot player before conclusion of play. By far the most popular of these gaming machines are the video poker machines. Video poker machines will be discussed in the next chapter.

The most appealing aspect of the slot machine is its simplicity. No knowledge or skill is required to play. Just put your money in the machine and push the button. In fact, in order to appeal to sentimental old-timers, some casinos still offer slot machines with steel arms that can be used to activate the machine. However, although there are also some machines that simulate the sound of coins dropping into a coin tray when credits are recorded, coins are no longer used. Instead, transactions are conducted with green money and credit memos that must be taken to a cashier's cage or a cashing machine. A cautionary note, never leave a machine for even a short break with credits on the machine. Anybody who sees that there are credits on the machine can hit the "Cash-Out" button and walk away with your hard-earned winnings.

Another attractive feature of the electronic slot machine is that it can be played for as little as a penny, but still offers the hope of a very large payout. However, especially for the smaller denomination machines, multiple coins must be committed on each play in order to qualify to win one of the large payouts. For example, on some penny machines, it is possible to commit more than two dollars on a single play.

The first question that any person who is considering playing a slot machine for the first time is likely to ask: "Is it really possible to win money on a slot machine?" The answer is yes and no. In the short run, it is definitely possible to win. In the long run, it is impossible. In order to explain, it would probably be best to tell you how a slot machine actually works.

How Slot Machines Work

Each slot machine contains a computer chip known as a random number generator (RNG), that controls the amount a machine will pay out. If the RNG is programmed to pay out 90% for each 100 plays (or spins) on a $1 machine, the machine will pay out $90 (or issue credits valued at $90). It is important to note that the $90 is only an average. It is possible that after 100 spins, you could have won thousands, even millions of dollars. It is also possible that after 100 spins, you could have absolutely zero dollars. Although either extreme is highly unlikely, it is obvious that if you continue to play long enough, you should expect to end up with 90% of nothing because the house advantage, be it 2% or 25%, will eventually grind you down. It is important to keep this in mind. Theoretically, in the long run slot machines cannot be beaten. However, it is also possible that if someone hits a huge multi-million dollar mega-jackpot on a slot machine, he may not live long enough to put all of his winnings back into a machine. Obviously, this is also true of the state lottery.

Most states regulate the minimum payout on slot machines. For example, in Nevada, the minimum payout is 75%. In New Jersey, the minimum is 83%. However, due to competition from other nearby casinos, in both Nevada and New Jersey, the average slot machine payout exceeds 90%. Although actual figures are not available, this is believed to be higher than the payout rate at most casinos in other areas.

Information regarding actual slot machine payouts is a closely guarded secret within the industry. However, data gleaned from various trade publications indicates that the vast majority of slot machines in American casinos pay out between 85% and 95%. As might be expected, because the popular smaller denomination machines take up as much space, and cost as much to maintain, as the larger denomination machines, the larger denomination machines generally have higher payout rates. However, due to differences in management objectives, payout rates may vary considerably from casino to casino, even between casinos that may be in relatively close proximity. For example, payout rates for casinos on the Las Vegas strip tend to be lower than casinos in outlying areas of the city.

Casinos in outlying areas of Las Vegas generally cater to a regular clientele of knowledgeable local residents. Cognizant of the need to develop and maintain a long-term relationship with this fairly stable customer base, managers of such casinos tend to be as generous as possible. In contrast, managers of casinos on the Las Vegas strip, where costs are much higher, and whose customers tend to be largely transient tourists and conventioneers who may never again set foot on the premises, tend to be less generous. For this same reason, slot machines in such places as convenience stores, supermarkets, and airports catering to traffic that just happens to be on the premises also tend to be less generous than those that are in a casino where the management is striving to develop a steady clientele of slot players.

Misconceptions About Slot Machines

One of the most persistent misconceptions about slot machines is that they are programmed to pay out on some vague pattern. Therefore, according to this misconception, a machine that has just paid a big jackpot will not pay out another jackpot anytime soon because it is "not due." This is totally incorrect. The RNG that controls the machine is a computer chip with no memory. The RNG randomly and continuously selects numbers without regard to the result of any previous play. Each number corresponds to a set of symbols that will appear in the window of the slot machine if that number happens to be selected. However, the symbols that appear in the window are strictly for show. Your fate was actually determined in the microsecond that the RNG selected your number. This means, barring any malfunction, a slot machine that has just paid out a huge jackpot is as likely to pay out another jackpot on the next spin as any other machine in the casino.

Another common misconception about slot machines is what I call the "I almost hit the jackpot" misconception. For example, if a huge jackpot will be paid if a diamond icon appears in each of the five windows on the machine, the appearance of a diamond in each of the first four windows may not actually be a near-miss because the number that resulted in the appearance of the four diamonds might have been millions removed from the actual number that would have resulted in the appearance of a diamond in each of the five windows. However, such "near-misses" do make for good story telling and definitely do help generate enthusiasm for such machines.

Another misconception about slot machines is that the management can readily adjust the payout rate. A commonly held misconception is that this is often done in order to improve the payout rate on weekdays, when business is slow, and reduce the payout rate on weekends and holidays when traffic is heavy. This thinking is also incorrect. In order to change the payout rate on a machine, it will be necessary to change the RNG. This will require the services of a skilled factory technician. Also, in most cases, the prior approval of a regulatory commission will be required.

Selecting the Right Machine for You

Slot machines are relentlessly negative expectation devices. Therefore, in theory, in the long-run it is impossible to win on these machines. However, for some people, the long-run can be a very long time. Some year ago, after playing only a few minutes in a Las Vegas casino, a college student won $10.9 million on a $1 progressive slot machine. Since continued play will result in a payout of approximately 93%, it is probable that the young man will not live long enough to put all that money back into the slots.

Because slot machines are negative expectation devices, they should be played for entertainment only. Entertainment means enjoyment. It is not fun to worry about how you are going to make the next mortgage payment. It is therefore important to make a wise choice when deciding which machine you will play and how much money you will spend playing that machine.

For most slot players, the first consideration is affordability.

Based on the assumption that a player will play at the rather leisurely pace of approximately ten spins per minute, the following table shows the expected average cost for each hour of play at a typical American casino.

Approximate Hourly Cost Table

Denominations	5¢	25¢	$1	$5
Total Funds Committed *(600 times denomination)*	$30	$150	$600	$3000
Expected Payout Amount	$24.90	$135	$558	$2880
Assumed Payout Rate	83%	90%	93%	96%
Expected Hourly Cost	$5.10	$15.00	$42.00	$120.00

"Expected Hourly Cost" figures that are shown above are approximations that are based on the assumption that one unit will be committed on each play.

On most slot machines, the payout rate will increase if played for more than one unit. This, however, is not true for all machines. Before playing a machine for multiple credits, compare payout amounts that are shown on the payout table. For example, on a machine that may be played for one, two or three credits, if the payout amounts for three credits are not more than three times greater than payout amounts for one credit, the payout rate is not increasing. There is, therefore, no advantage in playing the machine for more than one credit at a time.

Most writers recommend that when playing a slot machine that pays out at a higher rate when played for multiple credits, the machine always be played for maximum credits. Such advice is misleading and can be dangerous to the pocketbook. If a machine is played for multiple credits, "Expected Hourly Cost" can be expected to increase because the payout rate will not increase sufficiently to offset the larger amount that will be committed. In other words, for any given period of time, a person playing a quarter machine for multiple credits can be expected to lose more money than a person who has been playing a quarter machine for one credit. Also, a person who has been playing a $5 machine for any number of credits can be expected to lose more money than either of the players who have been playing the quarter machines. In summary, be aware that while it may be fun to "chase" the big jackpot, the cost will probably be high.

For most slot machines, the increase in payout rates is entirely the result of an inflated payout for the largest payout (the jackpot) on the machine. For example, the top line of one machine at a nearby casino shows the following payouts:

One Credit	Two Credits	Three Credits
2,000	4,000	28,000

A machine such as this should be played for either one credit or three credits. In either case, the amount that you commit should be consistent with your pocketbook and your objective. If your objective is to relax and play for a while, play one credit. If you want to gamble and go for a big payoff, play three credits. However, if such is the case, perhaps a progressive jackpot machine might be more suitable for you. Read on.

In deciding which machine to play, one of the most important considerations is the payout rate, which is the ratio of the amount of money that a machine will pay out in relation to the amount that the machine will take in. Obviously, the higher the payout rate, the more advantageous for the player. However, equally as important as the payout rate is the manner in which the payout is structured.

There are basically two types of slot machines in casinos. A "flat top" is a machine in which the jackpot is always a fixed amount. A "progressive" is a machine in which the jackpot increases as the number of plays increase subsequent to payment of the last jackpot.

A progressive jackpot machine may be an independent machine in which the amount of the jackpot is based on the receipts of that one machine or a combined jackpot machine in which the jackpot is combined for all similar machines in the casino. There are also progressive jackpot machines in which all similar machines within an entire city or state are connected. A jackpot for one of these city or statewide "Mega-Jackpots" can amount to millions of dollars. The size of the jackpot for an independent jackpot machine is shown in a meter on the machine. For combined jackpot machines, the size of the jackpot is usually shown on a huge flashing sign above a cluster of machines.

Because the chances of hitting a progressive jackpot, especially a statewide mega-jackpot, are extremely remote, but the payout for the jackpot is considered in the payout rate for each machine, for most casual slot players, a flat top machine will probably offer more "bang for the buck." There are, however, sometimes exceptions for independent jackpot machines. Occasionally, a jackpot for one of these independent jackpot machines will increase to such a level that it might be worth playing because I have seen machines for which the jackpot was much larger than for similar machines in the casino. If you can afford it, such a machine might offer good value.

Finding Loose Slot Machines

Any moderately knowledgeable video poker player can determine which machines are the most favorable by comparing payout tables that can be found on the machines (see the next chapter). Unfortunately, no such information is made available to slot players. Although broadly general information on this subject is published in such publications as *Strictly Slots* and *Casino Player,* payout data on individual slot machines is closely guarded within the various casinos. In fact, unless you are among a very privileged few, it is quite unlikely that you will ever encounter anyone in the casino who even has access to such data because access to such information will always be limited to key personnel. Information of this type is definitely not shared with employees who work on the casino floor, so don't bother to ask one of the attendants in the area to point you to a loose machine.

Although I cannot give you clues on how to find the loosest slot machine in a particular casino, I can give you a clue on how to find the casino that has the most generous slot machines in your area. It is known that casinos tend to view slot machines and video poker machines in the same light. In fact, in every casino that I have been to, these two types of machines are intermingled throughout the casino and are under the jurisdiction of the same person (the slot manager) who has a combined profit objective for all gaming machines in the casino. It therefore follows that casinos with video poker machines that pay out generously will probably also have slot machines that pay out generously. If you live in an area that is served by a large number of casinos, I would encourage you to shop around, because in conducting research for this book, I compared payout rates on video poker machines at numerous casinos in Nevada and southern California. I learned that there can be fairly significant differences between the various casinos.

Slot Tournaments

Many of the larger casinos sponsor regular daily, weekly, or monthly slot tournaments. These tournaments come in all sizes and shapes. Some are high stakes invitation-only tournaments that may include lodging, meals and complimentary gifts. Others are tournaments that are open only to participants at a convention or reunion. However, the vast majority of slot tournaments are open to the public. Because these tournaments are generally intended as promotional rather than revenue-producing activities, entry fees tend to be low and the payout rates high. In fact, because some of these tournaments are subsidized by the casino and pay out more than 100% of receipts, they can be among the best bargains that are available in the casino. A few casinos even sponsor free mid-week tournaments for senior citizens. Prizes for such tournaments generally consist of small cash prizes or coupons that can be used in casino restaurants and gift shops.

If interested in playing in a slot tournament, check with the concierge or promotion desk when entering the casino. There is a word of caution, however, most slot tournaments are single-session tournaments with the player (or players) having the most credits on their machine after the session sharing in the tournament pool. However, some tournaments are multiple-session tournaments with the winners from preliminary sessions progressing to a final session. Before entering a tournament, make sure that you will be available to participate in such a final session in the event that you are fortunate enough to qualify for the finals.

It is a generally accepted fact that there is absolutely no skill involved in playing a slot machine. However, there is a small measure of skill involved in playing in a slot tournament because in a slot tournament, the ability to play rapidly is a factor.

Slot tournaments are played on machines that record credits for winning combinations, but do not make deductions for the number of spins. Since it is obvious that the greater the number of spins, the greater the opportunities to qualify for credits, it is advantageous to play as rapidly as possible. Many tournament players attempt to get the maximum number of spins by sitting in front of the machine with their right hand above the play button, mindlessly hitting the button as rapidly as possible. This may not result in getting the maximum number of spins because in general, slot machines will not begin the next cycle until the current spin has been completed. Although there may be slight differences in the timing devices on various machines, it is recommended that you keep your finger on the play button and push down as soon as the previous spin is completed.

Video Poker Machine Layout

12. Video Poker

By far the most popular video gaming machines in American casinos are the video poker machines. These machines are based on Five-Card Draw, an old American card game that was very popular with poker players until Texas Hold'em was introduced to casinos in the last half of the twentieth century. We will therefore begin this chapter with a very brief explanation of how Five-Card Draw poker is played.

Five-Card Draw begins with each player being dealt five cards from a standard 52-card deck. After a round of betting, players who have remained in the game are given an option. They may retain their original five cards or replace one or more of their cards. After another round of betting, players turn over their cards and the player with the strongest poker hand wins the money that was in the pot. Unlike draw poker, in video poker, players do not compete against each other, but against the casino.

Poker hands are ranked according to the table on page 69. The rank (strength) of a poker hand is based on the frequency with which that hand will appear when randomly dealt from a standard 52-card deck. The less frequent the hand the higher it is ranked. From these frequencies, shown on page 69, approximate odds for each kind of hand can be computed. The next table re-states the names and frequencies of poker hands with the addition of the odds against the hand occurring.

Frequency of Poker Hands

Hand	Number	Approximate Odds
Royal Flush	4	649,700 to 1
Straight Flush	36	72,200 to 1
Four of a Kind	624	4,160 to 1
Full House	3,744	690 to 1
Flush	5,108	510 to 1
Straight	10,200	250 to 1
Three of a Kind	54.912	46 to 1
Two Pair	123,552	20 to 1
One Pair	1,098,240	1.37 to 1
No Pair	1,302,540	1 to 1

Total Possible Hands   2,598 960

According to these figures, when five cards are randomly dealt to a player, there are 2,598,960 possible hands (five-card combinations). Since only four of these combinations will constitute a royal flush, the chances of being dealt a royal flush are only one in 649,740. If the initial five cards constitute a royal flush, the player is said to have a "pat" royal flush. If the player must exchange one or more of his original cards in order to complete the royal flush, the player is said to have a "draw" to a royal flush.

Although the possibility of being dealt a pat royal flush is extremely remote, the possibility of making a royal flush increases substantially when a player is allowed to draw to the royal flush. Nevertheless, making a royal flush is always an extreme long shot when playing Five-Card Draw poker unless wild cards are used. More on the subject of wild cards will come later.

With the exception of possibly the cruise ships that operate in international waters, the five cards that appear on the screen when a player pushes the "Deal/Draw" button on a video poker machine simulates strictly the actual playing of Five-Card Draw poker with a freshly shuffled deck of cards. Therefore, the possibility that a royal flush will appear on the screen when a player pushes the button for the draw is also one in 649,740.

Since, as in actual draw poker, video poker players are also allowed to "draw" to the royal flush, the chance of actually making a royal flush also increases substantially. With optimal play, it is estimated that a royal flush will be made on a video poker machine once in approximately every 40,000 plays.

There are a bewildering variety of video poker machines in the casinos. In fact, there is even a machine that allows a player to play as many as 100 hands simultaneously. However, in the interest of clarity and simplicity, this book will concentrate on machines that provide for playing only one hand at a time. However, the strategy concepts contained herein are generally applicable to machines that provide for playing many hands simultaneously.

How to Play Video Poker Machines

The oldest and still the most popular games that are being played on casino video machines are "Jack or Better" and "Bonus Poker." Because most video gaming machines provide for playing non-poker games as well as several variations of five-card poker, the controls can be quite complex. There are also differences between various manufacturers. However, controls that relate to the playing of poker are usually very similar on all machines and appear essentially as shown in the figure on page 118.

Hit the "Help" button to summon an attendant. This is usually done to resolve a problem with the machine, but can also be used to get information on a new machine.

Hit the "Cash Out" button to print a credit memo that can be cashed at a cashier's window or a cash machine when you are finished playing.

Hit the "Bet One" button when you wish to play one credit on each hand. On most machines, if you wish to play more than one credit, it will be necessary to hit the button one additional time for each additional credit that you wish to commit. There is usually a light on the machine that will indicate the number of credits that are being committed on each play.

A "Hold/Cancel" button will be located below each card that

appears on the screen. Hit the button that is below each card that you wish to retain. "Hold" or "Held" will appear on the screen below each card that you wish to retain. If you mistakenly hit the wrong button, hit the button again and the sign on the screen will disappear. A word of caution, if you wish to retain all your original cards, you must hit all five "Hold/Cancel" buttons before hitting the "Deal/Draw" button to complete play on the hand. Failure to hit and hold each of the five cards can be disastrous because this could result in the voiding of a winning hand. On most video machines, touching the image of the card on the screen will also select cards that will be retained. I personally find this to be easier and more convenient than fumbling around with a bunch of buttons.

Hit the "Deal/Draw" button to (1) start play or (2) change cards on the screen after you have determined which cards you wish to retain.

Hit the "Bet Maximum Credits" button if you wish to commit the maximum number of credits on each play. This may also be accomplished by hitting the "Bet One" button the appropriate number of times.

Jacks or Better

As the title implies, for Jacks or Better, a player must have at least a pair of Jacks in order to qualify for a payout. Since this is the oldest and most popular form of video poker, we will begin with a discussion and analysis of Jacks or Better.

Because video poker hands are based on a random deal of an actual deck of cards, the true odds of making each hand can be mathematically determined. Since video poker players are competing against the casino, the casino must get its house advantage by paying out slightly less than true odds. Shown is an actual payout table from a Jacks or Better video poker machine.

Jacks or Better 8/5 Payout Table

	1 Coin	2 Coins	3 Coins	4 Coins	5 Coins
Royal Flush	250	500	750	1,000	4,000
Straight Flush	50	100	150	200	250
Four of a Kind	25	50	75	100	125
Full House	8	16	24	32	40
Flush	5	10	15	20	25
Straight	4	8	12	16	20
Three of a Kind	3	6	9	12	15
Two Pair	2	4	6	8	10
Pair of Jacks (or better)	1	2	3	4	5

The above table is for a flat top machine with a fixed jackpot of 4,000 credits. This means that on a $1 machine, the maximum payout will always be $4,000. However, in order to qualify for a chance to win the $4,000, the player will have to commit five credits ($5) on each play. Because the payout table provides for the payment of 8 credits if a player makes a full house and 5 credits if a flush is made when playing one credit, this table is known as an 8/5 table.

There are also progressive jackpot machines for which the jackpot can substantially exceed the 4,000 credits that are shown above. If such a progressive jackpot increases to approximately 8,800 credits, it is estimated that with skillful play, a machine with an 8/5-payout table will become a positive expectation instrument. Most writers on this subject therefore recommend that such a machine always be played for maximum credits. For recreational players, this advice may be dangerously flawed because it frequently leads to players playing beyond their means.

A machine with a large jackpot has become a positive expectation device only because of the large payout for the royal flush. However, even with skillful play, the royal flush is an extreme long shot. Therefore, playing for the royal flush can lead to disaster. There is no doubt that playing a machine with a large progressive jackpot for five credits makes more sense than playing that same machine for four credits. However, my advice is to always play judiciously within your comfort level. if you are a recreational player who is not comfortable committing $5 on each spin, a 9/6 machine that can be played for $1 is probably more suitable for you than an 8/5 machine with a large progressive jackpot.

For the knowledgeable casino patron, video poker machines have two distinct advantages over the regular slot machine. First, they offer games of skill. Therefore, by skillful play, the astute player can improve his chances of winning. Second, unlike on a regular slot machine, it is easy to determine which machine is the most favorable. The following table shows the amounts payable when playing Jacks or Better for one credit.

Typical Jacks or Better Payout Tables

Hand	9/6 Table	8/5 Table	7/5 Table	6/5 Table
Royal Flush	250	250	250	250
Straight Flush	50	50	50	50
Four of a Kind	25	25	25	25
Full House	9	8	7	6
Flush	6	5	5	5
Straight	4	4	4	4
Three of a Kind	3	3	3	3
Two Pair	2	2	2	2
Pair of Jacks (or better)	1	1	1	1

Except for the amount that will be paid when a royal flush is made while playing five credits (see the table on page 123), payment for all hands played for two, three, four, and five credits increase proportionally. Because the only differences between amounts that are paid are the amounts that are paid for a full house and flush, the various tables are referred to as 9/6, 8/5, 7/5 and 6/5 tables.

Since payout qualifying hands will appear with equal frequency on all Jacks or Better machines, it is obvious that a 9/6 machine is preferable to an 8/5 machine, an 8/5 machine is preferable to a 7/5 machine, etc. Before playing a video poker machine in a casino for the first time, it is recommended that you compare payout tables on a few machines in the casino before sitting down to play. It definitely pays to shop around. In one recent casino that I visited, I found that it was possible to get the benefit of a 9/6-payout table while playing for only $1 on a multiple-denomination machine that could be played for $1, $2, or $5 per credit. However, on machines in the casino that could be played for 25¢, 50¢ or $1 per credit, 7/5-payout tables were applicable. In other words, if you play the $1/$2/$5 machine for one credit at $1 per credit, you would be paid based on a 9/6 payout table. However, if you play the 25¢/50¢/$1 machine for one credit at $1 per credit, you would be paid based on a 7/5-payout table.

On almost all video poker machines, payout tables are displayed on the screen and can be brought forward by touching the appropriate icon on the screen.

Playing Strategy for Jacks or Better

As was indicated in the table on page 120, of the 2,598,960 five card combinations that might appear on the screen after a player hits the Play/Draw button to start play, less than half of the hands will include a pair. In fact, only 536,100 (21%) of the hands will include at least a pair of jacks, thereby qualifying for a payout. Prospects for success therefore rest heavily on the player's ability to make wise decisions when deciding how to draw to his hands. Following are a few hands with explanations that will hopefully provide some insight into the thought process that should go into determining how to play various hands on machines with the commonly used 8/5 and 7/5 payout tables.

HAND #1

K♦ Q♦ J♦ 10♦ 8♦

This hand is a flush, which according to the payout table qualifies for five credits. However, if the 8♦ is discarded, there is a possibility of making a royal flush by drawing the Ace of diamonds. Since after deducting the five cards that are shown above, there are 47 cards remaining in the deck, there is a one in forty-seven chance of making the royal flush. However, because the royal flush will pay 250 credits, which is 50 times more than the flush, the possibility of making the royal flush justifies discarding the 8♦. However, there are other considerations. The 9♦ will make a straight flush, which is worth 50 credits; any of the other seven diamonds will restore the flush; the non-diamond Aces and nines will make a straight, which would be worth four credits, and any King, Queen or Jack would make a pair that will qualify for one credit. Therefore, discarding the 8♦ would result in a huge positive expectation and is a "no-brainer." As is indicated in the table on page 123, if you are playing five credits, there is a much stronger incentive to discard the 8♦ and try to make the royal flush.

HAND #2

10♦ 9♦ 8♦ 6♦ 2♦

This is also a pat flush. If the 2♦ is discarded and is replaced by the 7♦, the straight flush is a possibility. However, a straight flush is worth only 50 credits, which is only 10 times the value of the current hand. Since the chance of making the straight flush is only 1 out of 47, it would be foolish to discard the 2♦.

HAND #3

7♦ 6♣ 5♦ 4♥ 2♣

If five random cards are dealt from a freshly shuffled deck of cards, there is only a 21% chance of getting five cards that will qualify for a payout. The chances are that five random cards dealt from the remaining cards in this deck are slightly higher than 21% because there is a higher ratio of Aces, Kings, Queens and Jacks in the remaining 47 cards.

If the 2♣ is discarded and replaced with an 8 or a 3, the result would be a straight, which will be worth 4 credits. Although there is only a 17 % (8/47) chance of making the straight, that would be the correct strategy for playing this hand. Note that if there is a gap in the four cards that you will be holding, such as 7♦ 6♣ 5♦ 3♥, the chance of making the straight will decline by 50% since there will be only four cards in the deck that will complete the straight. Do not draw one card to a straight unless all four cards that you are holding are consecutive cards, or at least three of the cards that you are holding are high cards that will qualify for a payout if paired. Example: K♦ Q♣ J♥ 9♠.

HAND #4

K♥ Q♦ J♦ J♣ 10♥

Although at first glance, some players may be tempted to discard one of the Jacks and draw to a straight, there is only a 17% (8/47) chance of making the straight, which will pay only four credits. Since the two Jacks constitute "money in the bank" and could improve to two pair, three Jacks, a full house, or even four Jacks, it would be much wiser to hold the two Jacks.

Categories of Starting Hands

With 2,598,960 possible starting hands, it is impossible, within the pages of this book, to provide specific recommendations for playing every hand. However, it is possible to provide general guidelines. The following guidelines are applicable for playing Jacks or Better on a machine that utilizes the popular 8/5 and 7/5 payout tables. For this purpose, the following abbreviations are used:

> RF= Royal Flush
> SF = Straight Flush
> HC = High Card (Ace, King, Queen and Jack)

Category 1: Hands that should always be played pat:

> Royal Flush (RF)
> Straight Flush (SF)
> Four of a Kind
> Full House

Category 2: Hands that should be played pat except under extraordinary circumstances:

> Flush - Break and draw one card only if you will be drawing to a RF.
> Straight - Break and draw one card only if you will be drawing to a RF, or a SF with four consecutive suited cards.

Category 3: Excellent drawing hands:

> Four cards to a RF (K♦ Q♦ J♦ 10♦)
> Three of a Kind
> Four cards to a high SF (K♠ Q♠ J♠ 9♠)
> Three consecutive cards to a RF (K♠ Q♠ J♠)
> Two pair
> Four cards to a low SF (9♣ 8♣ 7♣ 5♣)
> High pair (Aces, Kings, Queens, Jacks)

Category 4: Decent drawing hands:

> Four cards of same suit
> K-Q-J-10, not of same suit
> Q-J-10-9, not of same suit
> Pair smaller than Jacks
> Q-J-9 of same suit

Category 5: Marginal drawing hands:

> Two HC of same suit
> Four consecutive cards smaller than a Queen, not of same suit
> Three consecutive cards to a small SF
> Four cards to an Ace-high straight
> K-Q-J, not of same suit
> Two HC, not of same suit
> One HC
> Three small cards to a SF

Hands are listed above in order of preference. Therefore, if your original five cards include more than one of the hands that are listed above, retain the hand that is listed highest. An example:

Actual hand: K♣ K♦ Q♦ J♦ 10♥

Possible drawing hands: K♦ Q♦ J♦
                           K♣ K♦
                           K♦ Q♦ J♦ 10♥

Since K♦ Q♦ J♦ is listed higher than K♣ K♦ or K♦ Q♦ J♦ 10♥, the K♣ and 10♥ should be discarded. If it is not possible to draw to any of the hands that are listed above, discard all five cards.

Proper strategy for playing any video poker machine requires that consideration be given to the probability of making a particular hand and the potential payout. When played for more than one credit, the payout is proportional to the number of credits that were committed (see the table on page 123). The only exception is when a royal flush is made and the machine is being played for five credits. Since the payout for a royal flush can be proportionally much greater than for other hands, in some instances, it may be prudent to consider some changes in playing strategy. For example, in the preceding Classification of Hands, K♦ Q♦ J♦ 9♦, which is a one-card draw to a potential straight flush, is listed as a hand that is preferable to K♦ Q♦ J♦, which is a two-card draw to a potential royal flush. As is indicated in the table on page 123, when played for less than five credits, a royal flush will pay five times more than the straight flush. However, when played for five credits, a royal flush will pay off 16 times as much as the straight flush on a flat top machine. On a progressive jackpot machine, the payout could be far greater than on a flat top machine. Therefore, in spite of the long odds of making a royal flush by drawing to the K♦ Q♦ J♦, that may be the best choice.

Bonus Poker

Except that payment for certain hands (usually four of a kind) is enhanced, Bonus Poker is virtually identical to Jacks or Better. However, there are numerous variations of Bonus Poker. Following are some of the variations that are being offered in nearby casinos:

Bonus Poker   Bonus Poker Deluxe
Double Bonus Poker   Triple Bonus Poker
Double Double Bonus Poker   Triple Bonus Poker Deluxe

In the interest of simplicity and reasonable brevity, discussion will be limited to Bonus Poker and Double Bonus Poker.

The following table compares actual 7/5 payout amounts for Jacks or Better against payout amounts for Bonus Poker and Double Bonus Poker on a typical machine when played for one credit on a 25¢ machine.

Comparison of Payout Tables

	Jacks or Better	Bonus Poker	Double Bonus Poker
Royal Flush	250	250	250
Straight Flush	50	50	50
Four Aces	25	80	160
Four 2, 3, or 4	25	40	80
Four 5, 6, 7, 8, 9, 10, J, Q, K	25	25	25
Full house	7	6	9
Flush	5	5	6
Straight	4	4	4
Three of a Kind	3	3	3
Two Pair	2	2	1
High Pair (Ace, K,Q,J)	1	1	1

Note that for Bonus Poker, amounts that will be paid for four Aces, deuces, threes and fours have been increased. As an offset, the amount that will be paid for a full house has been reduced from 7 to 6.

For Double Bonus Poker, amounts that will be paid for four Aces, deuces, threes and fours have been doubled from that which will be paid for Bonus Poker. In addition, amounts that will be paid for full houses and flushes have also been increased. The only offset is that the amount that will be paid for two pair has been reduced from 2 to 1. At first glance, Double Bonus Poker may appear to be a bargain. In fact, it is not a bargain because two pair will appear on the screen far more frequently than the hands for which payouts have been increased (see the table on page 120).

When playing Double Bonus Poker, two pair is worth no more than one high pair. The only possible hand that can be made when drawing to two pair is a full house, a 4 out of 47 (8.5%) long shot that is worth only nine credits. However, four Aces are worth 160 credits. Therefore, if you have two pair with a pair of Aces as the high pair, the smaller pair should be discarded. All other hands with two pair should be retained.

As was noted above, there are now many variations of Bonus Poker. They all have one thing in common: they offer enhanced—sometimes greatly enhanced—payouts for certain hands that rarely appear on the screen, but compensate for those increases by reducing payouts for hands that will appear more frequently. However, of one thing you may be certain: the casino will always retain a house advantage. In fact, greatly enhanced payouts for hands that rarely appear on the screen are probably not in the best interest of the average recreational player because unless the player succeeds in making such a hand, he will be depleting his bankroll more quickly.

For those who prefer not to engage in too much heavy thinking when gaming, the maker of Game King machines has recently introduced video poker machines that automatically select cards that are recommended for holding. However, the player is given the option to make changes. These machines are programmed for five-credit play. If playing for less than five credits and a natural royal flush (meaning a royal flush without using any wild card) pays only 250 credits for each unit that is being bet, it would be wise to change some really long shot draws for a natural royal flush such as a King and 10. Also, you should check other machines of the same denomination in the casino that do not select cards for the player. It is quite likely that those machines will have a more favorable payout table. For the novice however, some practice time on a machine that selects cards might be wise because it will speed the learning process.

Joker Poker

In most home poker games, when a Joker is added to the deck, it is usually a wild card that may be used only as part of a royal flush, straight flush, flush, or straight. Otherwise, it is just another ace. In the video poker version, the Joker is a true wild card that can be used as any card that will maximize the strength of a hand.

Although there are some payout tables that also pay out for a pair of Aces or Kings, following is a typical payout table for Joker Poker.

Payout Table for Joker Poker

	1 Coin	2 Coin	3 Coin	4 Coin	5 Coin
Five of a Kind	400	800	1200	1600	4000
Royal Flush	100	200	300	400	500
Straight Flush	100	200	300	400	500
Four of a Kind	16	32	48	64	80
Full House	8	16	24	32	40
Flush	5	10	15	20	25
Straight	4	8	12	16	20
Three of a Kind	2	4	6	8	10
Two Pair	1	2	3	4	5

As was noted earlier in this chapter, the thought process for deciding how to play a hand in video poker involves deciding how to maximize expectation based on the applicable payout table. With a hand such as Q♦ J♦ 10♦ 10♣ and Joker, there are two plausible alternatives.

Alternative #1: Discard the 10♣ and draw to the royal flush (by retaining the Q♦, J♦,10♦ and the Joker).

Alternative #2: Discard the Q♦ and J♦, thereby retaining the three of a kind.

If Alternative #1 is chosen, the possibilities are as follows:

Four cards (A♦, K♦, 9♦, 8♦.) will result in a royal flush or straight flush, both of which will be worth 100 credits, assuming that you are playing one credit. Since there are 48 cards remaining in the 53-card deck, the chances of making either of these hands are 1 in 12 (4/48).

Six other diamonds will result in a flush, which will be worth 5 credits.

Twelve cards (Any Ace, King, 9, or 8 of spades, hearts or clubs) will result in a straight, which will be worth 4 credits.

Eight cards (Q♥ Q♣ Q♠ J♥ J♣ J♠ 10♥ 10♠) will reconstitute three of a kind.

If Alternative #2 is taken, there is a 1 in 1128 chance of making five 10s (2/48 x 1/47= 2/2256 = 1/1128). The only other hands that are possible are four of a kind, which will pay 16 credits and a full house, which will pay 8 credits. Although five of a kind will usually pay four times more than either a royal flush or a straight flush, because the chance of making the five of a kind is almost 100 times greater, Alternative #1 is the clear choice, notwithstanding the fact that you will be putting at risk the two credits that you have already won for your three 10s.

The vast majority of poker hands that will appear on the screen when you push the Deal/Draw button are straightforward and virtually play themselves. However, there will always be hands that will justify some thought. You are not paying the casino by the hour for using their machine. In fact, you will undoubtedly be paying the casino less for the use of their machine if you give it some thought before deciding on your course of action.

Video poker strategy is not rocket science. There are only 52 (53 for Joker Poker) cards in the deck. You will be looking at five of those cards. Your task is to maximize the payout potential based on the payout table and the possibility of making any hands that can be made with the cards that you have been dealt. A computer will be helpful, but is not necessary. I am confident that with some practice, the "computer" that you were issued at birth is adequate to significantly improve your play if pointed in the right direction.

Deuces Wild

With four wild cards in the deck, all hands except the natural royal flush (a royal flush that does not include a wild card) and the hand that contains all four of the deuces, are greatly devalued. Following is a typical payout table for Deuces Wild:

Payout Table for Deuces Wild

	1 Coin	2 Coins	3 Coins	4 Coins	5 Coins
Natural Royal flush	250	500	750	1000	4000
Four Deuces	200	400	600	800	1000
Royal Flush (with wild card)	25	50	75	100	125
Five of a Kind	15	30	45	60	75
Straight Flush	9	18	27	36	45
Four of a Kind	4	8	12	16	20
Full House	3	6	9	12	15
Flush and Straight	2	4	6	8	10
Three of a Kind	1	2	3	4	5

Following are a few basic rules for playing Deuces Wild:

Rule #1: Never hold one card unless it is a deuce.

Rule #2: Never hold two pair. If you have been dealt two pair, discard one of the pairs.

Rule #3: Draw one card to any four cards to a natural straight, even an inside straight such as 8♦ 7♣ 6♥ 4♦.

Rule #4: If you have two deuces in your hand, draw one card only if you have (a) four of a kind or (b) a one-card draw to a royal flush. Otherwise, hold the two deuces and draw three cards.

Rule #5: Discard a deuce only if (a) you have four cards to a natural royal flush and (b) you are playing five credits on a progressive machine that will pay approximately 5800 credits if you succeed in making the natural royal flush. The reason is that the wild royal flush you already have is worth 125 credits and the odds of making the natural royal flush are 1 in 47 (47 times 125 equals 5875).

Multiple-play Video Machines

A fairly recent addition to the world of video poker is the multiple-play machine. This is a machine that allows a player to play as many as 100 hands simultaneously. However, since all multiple-play machines operate in a similar manner, in the interest of simplicity, we will limit discussion to machines that allow for the playing of a maximum of three hands at a time.

Play begins with three five-card hands being displayed on the screen in the following manner:

Multiple-play Video Poker Screen

If only one credit is committed, only the five cards at the bottom of the screen are in play. If two credits are committed, the bottom and middle hands are in play. If three credits are committed, all three hands are in play for one credit each. If four credits are committed, the bottom hand will be played for two credits and the upper two hands will be played for one credit each. If the maximum of 15 credits are committed, all three hands will be in play for five credits each.

When the Deal/Draw button is pressed, the five cards at the bottom of the screen will be displayed. After the player decides which of the cards he will retain and presses down on the appropriate Hold/Cancel button for each of the active hands, a similar card will appear immediately above the card that was held. After the player again presses down on the Deal/Draw button, each active hand will be randomly and independently drawing cards from different decks of cards. It is therefore possible to make three different winning hands on a single play. For example, if a player holds a pair of Jacks, he could conceivably make four Jacks on one of his hands, a full house on a second hand, and two pair on the third hand. If such were the case, the sum of the credits for the three winning hands would be added to the total credits that were already on the machine.

Casino managers love the multiple-play, multiple-denomination video machines because of their versatility. For example, on a 5¢/10¢/25¢ triple-play machine, a customer can play the machine for as little as 5¢ or as much as $3.75 (5 x 3 x 25¢). They also like the fact that many players will commit five credits on each of the three hands.

Because they know that most players are committing far more than the minimum on each play, casino managers tend to be generous on their payouts. This may create attractive opportunities for the astute recreational player. During a recent visit to a nearby Indian casino, I noticed that when playing Jacks or Better at the 25¢ level on a regular machine, a 7/5 payout table was applicable. However, in the same casino, there were 25¢/50¢/$1 machines with 9/5 payout tables that could also have been played for as little as 25¢. As was stated earlier in this chapter, it pays to shop around, especially if you are in a casino for the first time.

One other attractive aspect of the multiple-play machine is that with its usually generous payout tables and modest minimum bets, it offers small stakes players a relatively inexpensive opportunity to try to hit the 4000 credit jackpot for making a royal flush. At the 5¢ rate, this will be as little as 75¢ for each play. Not only will the usually more generous payout table help you survive longer when you do have a chance to draw to the royal flush, but you will have several independent chances to make the always elusive royal flush.

One closing thought on video poker. As was indicated earlier, it is a simple matter to determine which are the most generous video poker machines. Since payout rates on video poker machines undoubtedly reflect the business philosophy of casino management, it probably would be safe to assume that a casino that has generous video poker machines also probably has generous slot machines. This is a factor that should be considered if you prefer video poker, but your spouse prefers the slots or vice versa.

Other Video Games

Blackjack and keno are two other video games that are commonly offered in casinos. Unfortunately, both have serious drawbacks. In general, the problem with video blackjack is that these machines usually pay only even money, rather than 3 for 2 when the player makes a blackjack, and do not allow the splitting of pairs or doubling down with a 10 or 11. Without these features, the casino has such a large house advantage that video blackjack is probably not worth considering.

The problem with playing keno on a video machine is that the game you will be playing is keno and keno has some of the longest odds and poorest payouts in the casino. The one favorable feature of video keno is that the smaller denomination machines offer the opportunity to pursue a relatively large payout for as little as five cents. However, the house advantage on these bets will always be huge. For further details, the reader is referred to Chapter 10 on keno.

Part IV

Competitive Games

The Sports Book

Horseracing

Casino Poker

13. The Sports Book

Although many American casinos have off-track betting lounges, only casinos in Nevada have lounges where bets may be made on sporting events other than horseracing. The reason is that tribal casinos must comply with state laws, and Nevada is the only state that has made it legal for casinos to accept bets on such sporting events as football, basketball and baseball. Nevertheless, although it is actually illegal for casinos to accept bets on these events, due to the overwhelming popularity of sports betting in America, the sports pages of most American newspapers provide readers with the latest betting lines on major sporting events.

The Point Spread

On sporting events such as football and basketball, in which a relatively large number of points are scored, a point spread system is generally used. With this system, the stronger of the two teams gives (or lays) the weaker of the two teams a specified number of points. For example, if the Green Bay Packers are favored to beat the Chicago Bears by 6 points, it will be indicated in the following manner

			Points
GREEN BAY	—	Chicago +6	42

The favored team is always listed to the left and capital letters are generally used to denote the home team. In some newspapers, the game may be listed in the following manner:

		Points
GREEN BAY -6 — Chicago		42

This should cause no confusion because all you need keep in mind is that the favorite is always listed to the left and the points always go to the underdog. In some cases, you will find "PK," which means "Pick'em," rather than a number between the two teams. This means that there is no betting favorite and the game is rated as a toss-up. You pick the favorite. The figure of "42" under "Points" is used for the over/under betting and is discussed later in this chapter.

Nevada casinos, as well as clandestine bookies in other states, take bets on professional sports as well as the more popular college sports. However, since the overwhelming bulk of the betting is on football, basketball, and baseball, we will concentrate on these three sports.

With point spread betting, you will be required to lay 11 to 10 on all bets whether you wish to bet the favorite or the underdog. This means if you give the bet taker $11 and win the bet, you will receive $21 and will have a profit of $10. However, if you lose the bet, you will have a loss of $11.

In order for a bettor who has bet on the favorite to win his bet, the favorite must beat the underdog by more than the point spread. In such cases, the favorite is said to have "beaten the spread." Therefore, in the above example, Green Bay must beat Chicago by more than 6 points. If Green Bay wins by exactly 6 points, the bet is a "push" and the $11 that the bettor had wagered is refunded. If Green Bay loses the game or wins by less than 6 points, the bet is lost. Therefore, in order to eliminate the need to refund bets, the point spread is frequently stated in half points. If this had been done in the above example, Green Bay would have been listed as either a 5 1/2 point or a 6 1/2 point favorite.

As was stated earlier in this book, casinos are not in business to gamble. They are in business to make money. Therefore, the ideal situation for the casino is to have an equal amount of money being bet on each of the two teams because this will insure a "win" for the casino, assuming that a half-point spread had been established. For example, if a total of $110,000 is bet on the Green Bay Packers and $110,000 is bet on the Chicago Bears, $210,000 will be paid to winning bettors and the casino will pocket $10,000 (4.55%) of the $220,000 that had been bet on the two teams. This 4.55% represents the house vigorish, usually referred to as the "juice" that the bettor must overcome in order to be a winner when betting at the sports book. To put it more clearly, since you are laying 11 to 10 on each bet that you make, in order to break even, you must win 11 of every 21 bets that you make, which is a win rate of 52.38% (11/21= 0.5238). This result is summarized as follows:

11 Winning bets @ $10	$110 Won
10 Losing bets @ $11	$110 Lost
21 Total Bets	-0-

At this point, it should be noted that the professional bookmaker who establishes the point spread is not trying to establish a point spread that reflects the relative strength of the two teams. His objective is to establish a point spread that will result in an equal amount of money being bet on each of the two teams. In other words, his sole concern is how the betting public will bet on the game. This means that when a bettor places a bet at a sports book, he is really not competing against an objective professional bookmaker, but against the general betting public with all its emotional attachments and biases. This will sometimes create favorable betting situations for the astute observer because the general public has a tendency to bet sentimental favorites, thereby making a team that should, by any objective criteria, be an underdog into a betting favorite. Many veteran sports bettors also try to get an edge by obtaining last minute injury reports on key players from 24-hour news programs and then placing bets before the injury is reflected in the point spread. Incidentally, casinos do sometimes make last minute changes to the point spread in order to try to balance amounts that are being bet on a game. However, the point spread for any bets that have already been made will not be changed.

The Over/Under Bet

Another popular sports bet is the "Over/Under Bet" in which a wager is made on the total number of points that will be scored by both teams during a game. In the example given in the section on point-spread bets, a point total of 42 was indicated for a game between the Green Bay Packers and the Chicago Bears. By laying odds of 11 to 10, the bettor may wager that the total number of points that will be scored in the game will be over 42 or under 42. If a total of 42 points are scored, the bet will be a push and all bets will he refunded. As with point-spread bets, half-points are also sometimes used in order to avoid the possibility of pushes.

The Money Line Bet

Because relatively few runs are scored in baseball games, instead of the point spread, the money line betting system is used for major league baseball games. The betting line, which is also sometimes used for other sports, including football and basketball, usually appears in the following form:

New York Yankees — 170   SEATTLE MARINERS +160

As with the point spread, the favorite is shown on the left and the home team is indicated by the use of capital letters. If the two teams are shown on separate lines, the favorite is listed above the underdog.

Data shown above indicates that the NY Yankees are a heavy favorite over the Mariners because a bettor that wishes to bet on the Yankees must lay $170 in order to win $100. However, the bettor that wishes to bet on Seattle stands to win $160 on his $100 wager.

Some sports books and newspapers present this very same data in a form that looks entirely different.

New York Yankees — SEATTLE 8 - 8 1/2

This indicates that (a) a $5 bet on the underdog will win $8 and (b) $8.50 must be bet on the favorite in order to win $5. Note that 8/5 = 160/100 and 8 1/2 /5= 170/100.

The opening line on a baseball game depends heavily on the scheduled starting pitchers because obviously, if the starting pitcher for the team of your choice is a Randy Johnson or a Roger Clemens in his prime, your chances are going to be much better than if the starting pitcher is an unknown rookie that has just been called up from the minor leagues. Sports books, therefore, usually offer an option. If one or both of the scheduled pitchers is unable to start, you will have an option of (a) having your bet automatically cancelled and your wager refunded or (b) the wager will stand with the odds being adjusted as appropriate by the sports book.

The Parlay Bet

Although the point-spread, over/under and money-line are by far the most popular types of bets that are made in the sports betting lounge, there are numerous other ways of betting on sporting events. The most popular of these other bets is the parlay. A parlay is a bet in which two or more separate bets are combined into a single wager. For example, a bet might be made that on a given Sunday, the Dallas Cowboys, Oakland Raiders, Green Bay Packers, and the Minnesota Vikings will all be winners. Normally, in order to win a parlay, all teams that were selected must actually win and a tie is treated as a loss. However, in some sports books, a tie is simply disregarded. In other words, if you had bet a four-team parlay and won on three of your bets, but tied on a fourth bet, the tie bet would he disregarded and you would be paid as if you had won a three-game parlay. Obviously, the difference between the two interpretations might be huge. Before betting a parlay, get clarification on this point.

The beauty of the parlay is that the potential payoff can be very big. The drawbacks are that it is very difficult to win a parlay, and the house advantage is huge, especially if more than three teams are selected. The following table provides a summary of the probability of winning a parlay consisting of even bets (bets between teams that have been rated even or have been made even with a point spread), the true odds, and the house edge.

Data on Parlay Bets

Teams Selected	Probability of winning	True Odds	Typical Payout	House Advantage
2	1 in 4	3-1	13-5	10.00%
3	1 in 8	7-1	6-1	12.50%
4	1 in 16	15-1	11-1	25.00%
5	1 in 32	31-1	22-1	28.12%
6	1 in 64	63-1	44-1	29.69%

In view of the fact that the house advantage on a single-game bet is only 4.55%, the house advantage on parlay bets is prohibitive, especially when betting on more than three games. Many weekend players cannot resist the temptation to make a "killing" on multiple-game bets. However, it would be far wiser to stick to the basic single-game bet and parlaying winnings yourself from one week to the next. For example, if you win $10 one weekend, bet the entire $21 (your original $11 bet, plus the additional $10 that you had just won) on one game the following week. In addition to avoiding the high house advantage that applies to parlay bets, this will have the advantage of having you betting on only your strongest picks of the week.

The Teaser

Closely related to the parlay is the "teaser." A teaser is essentially a multiple-game parlay with a lower payout. However, as compensation for the lower payout, the bettor is given points that may be distributed at the bettor's discretion. For example, assume that the actual betting line on a given Sunday is as follows:

DALLAS COWBOYS	—	NY Giants	+6
Oakland Raiders	—	DENVER BRONCOS	+6
Green Bay Packers	—	CHICAGO BEARS	+6

With a six-point teaser, the bettor may assign six points to the team of his choice in each of the three games. For example, if the bettor assigns the six points to each of the three underdogs, his revised betting line will be:

DALLAS COWBOYS	—	NY Giants	+12
Oakland Raiders	—	DENVER BRONCOS	+12
Green Bay Packers	—	CHICAGO BEARS	+12

The number of tease points is normally 6, 6 1/2 or 7, and payoffs vary. However, a two-game, six-point teaser is usually an even money bet, which means that on a winning $5 bet, the bettor will receive $10 (including the $5 that had been bet). This compares with the $18 (including the $5 original bet) that a winning parlay bettor would have received. However, it should be noted that in most sports books, the bettor must win on each game and a tie game will be treated as a loser.

Although many recreational bettors are tempted to make teaser bets because they like the idea of enhancing their chances of winning with a bet on a team that they want to bet, teasers are generally shunned by the "wise guys" (big-time professional sports bettors) because the payouts are too low and the risks too great, especially when considering that one bad bounce of the ball in any one of the games can ruin any otherwise solid multiple-game teaser bet.

Some Betting Tips

There are a virtually endless variety of bets that can be made at a sports book. Some, such as the number of strikeouts that will be recorded by a famous pitcher in an important baseball game, draw considerable interest. Others are as simple and inane as the result of the opening coin toss before the start of the Super Bowl, an 11 to 10 heads-or-tails bet. In general, as long as the sports book can generate enough action to balance the betting and insure a safe "juice," you can usually find a sports book that will take almost any bet. However, if you are looking for a big payoff on a long shot, such as the preseason chances of the Chicago Cubs to win the World Series, you can expect to pay a very substantial juice.

As noted earlier, bookmakers who establish betting lines for casinos are not trying to develop odds that reflect the actual strength of the competing teams. Rather, the objective of the bookmaker is to establish betting lines that will result in an equal amount of money being bet on each of the two teams. This creates opportunities for the knowledgeable sports bettor, because average sports bettors are inclined to bet with their hearts, not their heads. For example, assume that Notre Dame is traveling to Seattle to play the University of Washington Huskies in a very important football game that will have an important impact on national ratings, and all factors considered, the game should be rated as a dead-even "pick'em." The official betting line will almost certainly have Notre Dame rated as at least a slight favorite, because Notre Dame has a large national following, but Washington does not. The odds makers therefore know that if the game were rated as an even bet, the betting would heavily favor Notre Dame. Therefore, in order to encourage more betting on Washington, the odds makers will make Notre Dame at least a small favorite by giving Washington a few points.

Although actual figures are not available, it is generally estimated that sports books in Nevada account for no more than 10% of bets that are made on such sports as football, basketball, and baseball in the United States. Almost all the other bets are placed with clandestine bookies who operate in every corner of the country. Most of these bookies are believed to be independently operated and use betting lines that are established for Las Vegas casinos. However, in order to avoid the possibility of a disastrous loss that might result from uneven betting in their area of operation, local bookies normally make some changes in the point spread. As a result, significantly different point spreads may exist in different cities that are in relatively close proximity. For example, USC might be a three-point favorite over the University of California Golden Bears at a bookie in Los Angeles, but an even-money bet at a bookie in Oakland. If such a condition develops, and you bet $100 on the California Bears with a bookie in Los Angeles (you will have to give the bookie $110), and bet $100 on USC with a bookie in Oakland, the net financial result of the two bets will be as follows.

• **If USC wins the game by one or two points:**

    (1) You will win the bet that you had placed with the bookie in LA because although USC did win the game, they did not beat the point spread (three points). The bookie in LA will therefore pay you $210 and you will have won $100.

    (2) You will win the bet that you had placed with the bookie in Oakland and will also win $100. The net result of the two bets is that you will have won a total of $200.

• **If USC wins the game by exactly three points:**

    (1) You will push on your bet with the LA bookie.

    (2) You will win $100 on the bet that you made with the bookie in Oakland. The net result of the two bets is that you will have won $100.

• **If USC wins the game by more than three points:**

    (1) You will lose $110 on the bet that you had placed with the bookie in LA.

    (2) You will win $100 on the bet that you made in Oakland. The net result is that you will have lost $10 on the two bets.

• **If California wins the game, regardless of the score:**

    (1) You will win $100 at the LA bookie.

    (2) You will lose $110 at the Oakland bookie. The net loss on the two bets is $10.

This method of betting on both teams that are competing is sometimes referred to as betting on both sides of the spread or risking small to win big. Although usually much smaller, because of uneven betting between sports books, there are sometimes differences between sports books in Las Vegas.

Another opportunity to risk small and win big arises when the point spread changes substantially during the week. For example, assume that USC is scheduled to visit rainy Seattle to play the Washington Huskies in late November and open the week as a 13-point favorite. However, late in the week, it is reported that USC's all-American quarterback will be unable to play due to an injury that was sustained in practice and that the weather bureau is reporting that a sudden storm from the north Pacific is expected to drench Seattle over the weekend. As a result, USC is dropped from a 13-point favorite to a 9-point favorite. If you had already made a bet on Washington as a 13-point underdog, you will now be in a position to risk small and win big by placing a bet on USC as only a 9-point favorite because if USC wins the game by 10, 11, or 12 points, you will win both your bets.

There are approximately 250 Division I college basketball teams and almost as many Division I-A and Division II-A college football teams. Add to that, more than 100 professional sports franchises in the United States and Canada, and the magnitude of the professional odds makers task on establishing and updating daily betting lines becomes obvious. Odds makers are mere mortals. Occasionally, they will establish betting lines that are subject to serious question. Your task as an astute sports bettor is to find and capitalize on such betting lines. Here is one actual example.

In late August 2006, the sports pages of *USA Today*, one of the most highly respected sources of statistics and sports betting lines in the country, published its initial 2006 college football power rating. Also included in this same issue were the odds that various top teams would win the 2006 Bowl Champion Series (BCS) and finish the season as the #1-ranked college football team in the country. Some of the teams listed were:

Notre Dame	6-1
Ohio State	7-1
USC	10-1
Boise State	100-1
Arizona State	300-1

The BCS championship game, which normally matches the #1-ranked team in the country at the end of the regular season against the #2-ranked team was scheduled to be played in Glendale, Arizona, on January 8, 2007. One of the most important factors in determining the ranking of a college football team is the strength of that team's schedule during the regular season. Boise State is a member of the weak Western Athletic Conference (WAC) and their schedule did not include a single game against a team that was rated among the top 25 teams in any major preseason poll. It was therefore highly unlikely that Boise State would be invited to play in the BCS championship game even if they did finish their regular season unbeaten by whipping the likes of Sacramento State, Idaho and New Mexico State. In fact, Boise State did finish their regular season unbeaten and untied with a perfect 12-0 record. They then concluded the most successful season in the school's history by beating heavily favored Oklahoma in the Fiesta Bowl on January 1, 2007. However, Boise State had no realistic chance of winning the national championship because they had no chance of being selected to play in the BCS championship game.

On the other hand, Arizona State University, which was rated as one of the stronger teams in the highly regarded Pacific 10 Conference, did have a legitimate long shot chance of getting into the BCS championship game because they had a very favorable schedule, which included only one possible inclement weather game against Oregon State on November 4 and a decent, but not formidable, non-conference schedule. Therefore, at 300-1, Arizona State was a good long shot bet, especially since the BCS championship game was scheduled to be played in Glendale, Arizona, which is a short drive from the Arizona State campus. At 100-1, Boise State was a poor bet, notwithstanding the fact that as it turned out, Boise State did have what would prove to be an excellent team.

It is generally agreed by knowledgeable insiders that in the long run, 90% of men and women who bet regularly at a sports book are losers. Of course, the flip side is that 10% are winners, and that probably makes the sports book the closest thing to a beatable gambling venue in the casino. So how do you go about becoming one of the winners? Here are a few simple tips:

• **Limit your wagering to those sports, leagues and teams for which you have the greatest knowledge.** In order to overcome the juice, you need to be at least 4.55% smarter (more knowledgeable) than the average bettor in your betting pool. If you are a West Coast person, you are undoubtedly more familiar with teams, leagues, playing conditions, etc. on the West Coast than in other areas of the country. For example, because of greater differences in playing conditions in late season, the home field advantage is likely to be far more important for a crucial Pac 10 game between USC and Washington than a Big 10 game between Michigan and Ohio State. I do not mean to imply that if you are a West Coast person, you should never bet on a game between USC and Notre Dame. I mean that you should be more inclined to be betting on a Stanford-Oregon game than a game between Georgia and Alabama. Also, if you are a baseball fan in an American League city and are therefore more familiar with the American League than the National League, you will probably have a greater chance of success by betting on American League games than on National League games.

• **Try to avoid betting sentimental favorites.** Betting on your alma mater may be more fun, but may not be good for your pocketbook.

• **Limit the number of games that you are betting.** If you are an average football fan and are betting on a dozen college football games each week, you are probably betting several games on little more than a hunch. Hunch bettors tend to drown in juice.

• **Avoid multiple-game bets such as parlays and teasers.** By judiciously deciding when and where to place your bets, you will have a realistic chance of overcoming a 4.55% juice. In the long run, there is no way that you are going to overcome a 25-35% juice.

• **Shop the sports books.** There are sometimes small differences between odds offered by the sports books in Las Vegas. In a football game, the difference between 3 points and 3 1/2 will sometimes mean the difference between a win and a loss. Also, the differences between some preseason futures bets can be very big.

• **Look for special circumstances, especially late in the season, that may affect the score of a game.** For example, assume that Notre Dame, one of the top-rated college football teams in the country, is preparing to play Podunk Tech one week prior to playing USC, the #1-ranked team, and that Notre Dame is an overwhelming 36-point favorite over Podunk Tech. Since Notre Dame will have no incentive to run up the score against Podunk Tech, but would have an incentive to protect its best players and avoid revealing information to scouts from USC who will be watching the game, Podunk Tech and the points would be a bet that you might want to consider. Obviously, however, it would be wise to take into consideration the fact that others may feel the same way.

Somewhat similar circumstances occur in professional sports when teams are competing for postseason playoff berths. For example, assume that the Los Angeles Dodgers are competing against the New York Mets for the wild card slot on the last day of the season, and that the Mets have lost their game on the East Coast thereby clinching the playoff berth for Dodgers before the Dodger game, which was scheduled to be played on the West Coast, even begins. The Dodger game, which would have been the most important game of the season for the Dodgers had the Mets won, would now become a virtually meaningless exhibition game. The Dodgers would undoubtedly change their starting lineup for the last game in order to rest their best players for the playoffs, thereby greatly affecting the true odds on the game. Sports books handle such situations in several different ways. In many sports books, betting would be suspended pending completion of the first game. In other sports books, bets are taken only on the condition that the two scheduled starting pitchers actually start the game. In other cases, bets are accepted with the odds subject to change if the scheduled starting pitchers do not actually start the game.

For the wise money, there is an angle. If the Mets game was not completed when the Dodgers game began, the Dodgers will probably start their game with their best available players "just in case." However, if the Mets game is completed while the Dodgers game is in its early stages and the Mets have lost, the Dodgers will probably pull their starting pitcher and most of their other star players. A bet on the team that was scheduled to play the Dodgers might, therefore, have been a good bet.

Although this book is primarily about gambling in casinos, a cautionary note is in order for the 90% of sports bettors who place their bets with clandestine bookies outside of Nevada. From time to time, sports bettors have been unable to collect on their winnings bets because one of the clandestine sports betting operations was abruptly closed due to a criminal investigation. It is probably not wise, therefore, to place large bets with clandestine bookies, especially for futures bets. A lot can happen between the start of the baseball season in early April and the conclusion of the World Series in late October. Also, if you have a winning ticket from one of those clandestine bookies, be inclined to cash it in promptly.

One final word of caution. It is believed that the vast majority of "bet runners" who take bets for these clandestine bookies in various casinos and workplaces across the country are also placing bets with money that they receive as commissions from the bookies. In fact, many sports bettors finance their sports betting in this way. Although, in general, small-scale sports bettors usually get little attention from federal, state, and local police authorities, who periodically clamp down on illicit gambling activities, if you have been a bet runner, you might be seen as a possible conduit to information about higher figures in the bookie operation. This could lead to serious legal problems, including the loss of professional licenses, businesses, etc. Beware.

14. Horseracing

Many of the large casinos, particularly those in Atlantic City and Las Vegas, have off-track betting (OTB) lounges where bets are taken for major racetracks across the country. So that bettors might be able to follow the action, these lounges contain huge TV screens where images of several actual races are in progress, as well as corresponding tote boards. Since thoroughbred racing is by far the most popular form of racing, we will concentrate on thoroughbred racing.

Because many casino patrons may not be familiar with thoroughbred racing, we will begin this chapter with some basic definitions. Letters in parenthesis, shown next to some of the definitions, indicate abbreviations that are used in racetrack programs, as well as the *Daily Racing Form,* which will be on sale in the OTB lounge. The *Daily Racing Form* contains important details on every major race that is scheduled at an American racetrack and is an essential tool for any serious horseplayer. Separate editions of the *Daily Racing Form* are published for each region of the country. However, program data for most of the famous racetracks are included in all editions of the paper.

Types of Horses

Colt: Male, less than five years old.

Filly: Female, less than five years old, that has not been bred.

Gelding: Male that has been castrated. Colts that are difficult to handle are sometimes castrated in order to make them easier to handle.

Horse: To the general public, a horse is any specie of that graceful four-legged animal that is illustrated in the dictionary. At a racetrack, however, a horse usually means a male that is at least five years old and has not been castrated.

Maiden: Any male or female that has never won a race.

Mare: Female at least five years old. Also, refers to a female less than five years old that has been bred.

Types of Races

Allowance Race: A race for which weights carried by the horses depend on conditions that were established for that race. For example: Three-year olds: 117 lbs; More than three years old: 124 lbs; Non-winners for past year: 2 lbs deducted.

Claiming Race (CL): Each entrant has a claiming price at which any qualified horseman or woman can purchase the horse after the race.

Handicap Race (HC): A race for which the track secretary assigns weight that will be carried by each horse. Since owners may enter any handicap race, by paying the entrance fee, this is done in order to make the race more competitive.

Maiden Race (MDN): A race for horses that have never won a race.

Stake Race (STK): A race, usually for top two and three-year olds, that has a high entry fee. The most famous races such as the Kentucky Derby are stake races.

Bets on a Single Race

Win: Bettor collects only if the horse finishes first.

Place: Bettor collects only if the horse finishes first or second.

Show: Bettor collects only if the horse finishes first, second, or third.

Across the board: Three bets consisting of one win, one place, and one show that are purchased as a package.

Quinella: A bet in which the bettor must select the top two finishers, regardless of which of the two wins the race.

Exacta: A bet in which the top two finishers must be selected in the exact order of finish.

Trifecta:

A bet in which the first three finishers must be selected in the exact order of finish.

Superfecta:

A bet in which the first four finishers must be selected in the exact order of finish.

Bets on Multiple Races

Daily Double:

A bet in which the winner of two consecutive races must be selected. Usually, these are the first two races of the day.

Pick Three:

A bet in which the winners of three consecutive races must be selected.

Pick Six:

A bet in which the winner of six consecutive races must be selected. If there are no winners, payment is usually made to those who had correctly selected five winners, and a portion of the betting pool is added to the pool for the next day.

Most races are run over distances of five furlongs (one furlong equals 220 yards or 1/8 of a mile) to 1 1/8 miles, with the younger horses running the shorter races. The races are generally run over all on a portion of an oval, dirt track. However, at some of the larger racetracks, a few races are run on grass tracks that are laid out inside the main dirt track. According to tradition, races of less than a mile are stated in furlongs and races of a mile or more are stated in miles.

A separate pari-mutuel pool is set up for monies that are received for each type of bet. For example, monies received from bettors who had purchased win tickets are not commingled with monies that were collected from bettors who had purchased daily double tickets. Within each pari-mutuel pool, money that was collected from all bettors is pooled and paid out to those bettors who have winning tickets after all expenses, taxes, etc., have been deducted. In general, approximately 20% of the pool is deducted. Although this 20% deduction may not seem insurmountable to some, when considering the fact that this 20% is deducted for 9 or 10 races each session, the amount is very substantial. However, so is the cost of operating a racetrack.

The odds and the payout for a horse depend upon the number of bets that were made on the horse in relation to the number of bets that were made on the other horses in the race. The smaller the number of bets that were made on the horse that you had selected, the higher the odds and the potential payout. Conversely, the larger the number of bets that were made on your horse, the lower the odds and the smaller the potential payout. The odds will therefore continually change until the betting cages are closed just prior to the start of the race.

After completion of a race, official results and payouts will be posted on the tote board in the following manner:

	Post Position	Horse	Win	Place	Show
1st	6	Speedy Kay	12.20	8.20	4.20
2nd	1	Joe's Baby	5.60	3.20	
3rd	9	Speed Freak	3.60		

Payout amounts shown above are the amounts that will be paid to holders of winning $2 tickets. Normally, $2 is the smallest amount that may be bet at a racetrack. However, for a few difficult long shot bets, such as the Pick Six, a $1 bet might be accepted.

Payout amounts at racetracks are rounded down to the nearest ten cents. Any amount above ten cents, which is known as the breakage, is distributed according to applicable state law. In most cases, the racetrack retains the breakage. At this point, a word of caution is appropriate. Never discard a losing ticket until the results of a race have been declared official. In some cases, race results are changed because of a disqualification, such as when one horse improperly cuts in front of another horse.

The post position refers to the location of the horse in the starting gate. In the sample that was previously shown, Joe's Baby started in position 1, which is the position that is the closest to the inside rail, and Speedy Kay started in position 6, which is five positions to the right of Joe's Baby. Position 1 is the preferred position in a race because the closer to the rail, the smaller the circumference of the loop around the track. Therefore, horses that start on an outside track must run a slightly longer distance than horses that started the race on an inside track. As a result, horses that started the race on an outside track will try to pass and get in front of horses that started the race on an inside track in order to reduce the distance that they will be required to run.

In order to assist bettors in identifying their horse during the race, jockeys dress in bright, distinctive uniforms and caps that are noted in the racetrack program and the *Daily Racing Form.* Also, a clearly numbered saddle blanket, which indicates the post position is worn by each participant. These saddle blankets are in standard colors. For example, the blanket for a horse that is in post position number one will always be red; the blanket for the horse that is in post position number two will always be white, etc.

How to Select Your Horse

Based on such factors as the racing history of the horse, jockey, trainer, and owner; the length of the race, the assigned post position, the weight that will be carried, etc., the official track handicapper establishes the morning line which will serve as the opening odds when the betting windows open for each race. This morning line, which will appear in the track program, usually reflects quite realistically, the true odds at the start of the race. However, in the long history of thoroughbred racing, there has never been an official handicapper, professional though he or she may be, who was capable of consistently putting out a morning line that one could take to the bank. There are always far too many unpredictable variables. Nevertheless, the racetracks and OTB lounges are always full of amateur handicappers with their *Daily Racing Form*, official program, scratch-pad and hunches, who like to think that they can outguess the professionals. Rarely do they succeed. However, one of the main attractions of thoroughbred racing is the chance to beat the odds, the professional, and fellow amateur handicappers.

Some racetrack regulars try to get the edge on rival handicappers by getting inside information on such things as which horses have been running well in recent training sessions. However, a visitor to an OTB lounge normally would not have access to such information. So how should a casual handicapper in an OTB lounge select his horse? With the knowledge that the odds indicated in the morning line are usually realistic, probably the simplest and most logical method is to follow the odds on the tote board as bets are posted and then put your money on those horses that you might have been inclined to pick if the odds on those horses become favorable. For example, assume that based on your examination of what you consider to be relevant facts, you decide that "Got A Chance," which opened on the morning line at 5 to 1, might be a good bet. As the betting progresses, the odds on "Got A Chance" improve to 8 to 1. In the absence of any information that "Got A Chance" is not in top shape, this might be a good bet, perhaps for an "across the board" bet. Note that if you utilize this method of deciding which horses to pick, you probably will not be betting on every race. This just could be the most compelling aspect of this system.

15. Casino Poker

Due to the intricacies of poker and the variety of games that are being played, the poker room is undoubtedly the most challenging casino venue to analyze. However, because poker is the only game in the casino in which patrons do not compete against the house directly, and therefore do not have a consistent house advantage to overcome, the poker room may offer professionals the best overall opportunity to actually make a living in a casino. In fact, due to the recent explosion of interest in poker, the number of successful professional poker players is believed to have increased substantially in recent years. However, it is not the intent of the author to teach you how to join the ranks of these high-roller professionals. That would go far beyond the scope of this modest guide on how to enjoy yourself in a casino without losing your shirt.

This chapter was written with the assumption that the reader has already played some poker and is therefore familiar with the most basic fundamentals of the game. If you are not familiar with such basics as the strength of hands and the probability of making these hands, a review of the table of poker hands on page 69 and the table on page 120 on poker odds will be helpful before continuing further.

When exercising an option at a video poker machine, a player need consider only the mathematical probability of making a hand in the relatively simple game of Five-Card Draw poker against a potential payout table. In a casino poker room, a considerable variety of games are played and many of these games are quite complex. There are also numerous other factors that need to be considered at a poker table. In the interest of reasonable brevity,

I will therefore discuss in some detail only the game of Texas Hold'em, which is by far the most popular casino poker game. However, for the benefit of those who might be interested in delving further into the subject of poker, I strongly recommend *The Intelligent Guide to Texas Hold'em Poker, 2nd Edition* by Sam Braids. Unlike most poker books, which in the opinion of the author are grossly overpriced, this moderately priced 274-page paperback covers all the important aspects of the game. The book also includes an excellent recommended reading list that should be extremely useful to anyone who might be interested in a more detailed study of any specific aspect of poker.

Texas Hold'em

Texas Hold'em begins with each player at the table being dealt two cards face-down. These two cards are for the exclusive use of that player. Because other players at the table cannot see these cards, they are said to be "in the pocket." After a round of betting, three cards, which constitute what is known as the "flop," are turned face-up on the table. At this point, the three-card flop combined with the two pocket cards constitute each player's five-card hand. After a second round of betting, the dealer will turn a fourth card, which is known as the "turn" card, face-up on the table.

After a third round of betting, the dealer will turn a fifth card, which is known as the "river" card, face-up on the table. The five cards that the dealer has turned over on the table constitute what is known as the "board."

Following a fourth and final round of betting, players will show their two pocket cards and the player who has the best hand, using the five cards on the table and his two pocket cards, will win the pot. In some cases, the five cards that were turned face-up on the table will constitute a player's hand because neither of his two pocket cards can improve on the hand that is shown on the table. In such cases, a player is said to be "playing the board." Following is an example of when a player would be playing the board:

Player's pocket cards: K♦ K♠
Cards showing on the table: K♣ Q♦ J♥ 10♣ 9♦

In this example, the pocket Kings do not play, because three Kings is ranked lower than the King-high straight that is on the board. Note that if another player has an Ace, that player will have an Ace-high straight and that an Ace-high straight is the best possible hand that can be made with the cards that are showing.

Texas Hold'em is a game in which big cards, especially big pairs in the pocket, and the position of a player relative to the player who is serving as the dealer for the hand, are paramount. Position refers to the location of a player in relation to the player who is serving as the dealer for the hand. In the interest of clarity, hereafter in this chapter, any reference to the "dealer" will not refer to the casino employee who is actually dealing the cards, but the player who is the last player to receive his cards and is the last player to act on his hand.

Because the player who is in the dealer position has the advantage of acting on his hand last, the dealer position rotates around the table and is indicated by a distinctive "dealer" button that will be placed in front of the dealer by the casino employee who is dealing the cards. This "house dealer" is employed by the casino to deal the cards and monitor the action, but is not a player and serves only as an impartial observer.

The initial decision to play or fold a hand depends heavily on your position relative to the dealer and the strength of your first two cards. Position is extremely important because the later you will act, the more information you will be able to gather regarding the strength of your hand relative to the strength of hands that other players may be holding. Equally important is the fact that this positional advantage will continue throughout the hand. In other words, if you are the dealer and are therefore the last player to act after the flop, you will also be the last player to act for each subsequent round of betting.

Starting Hands

Texas Hold'em is played both as a limit game, in which the amount that may be bet is predetermined or as a no-limit game, in which, at any time, a player may bet any amount that he wishes to bet, provided of course, that he has that amount of money on the table. Although almost all TV poker programs feature high-stakes no-limit poker, the vast majority of actual casino poker games are limit poker games that are played for relatively moderate stakes. At this point, it should be mentioned that there are two different types of limit poker games. In a "fixed limit game," the amount that may be bet is a predetermined amount. For example, in a $3-$6 Texas Hold'em game, only $3 may be bet (or raised) during the first two rounds of betting, and only $6 may be bet during the last two rounds of betting. The only exception is if a player has less than the prescribed amount of money on the table. In this instance, the player may bet the amount that he has on the table.

In a "spread-limit game," a player may bet (or raise) any amount up to the betting limit. For example, in a $6 spread-limit game, at any time, a player may bet $1, $2, $3, $4, $5 or $6.

Following are categories of starting hands that are recommended for play in a limit Texas Hold'em game. Within each category are specific hands that are listed approximately according to strength. It should be noted, however, that the order in which hands are listed is subject to adjustment depending on the circumstances. For example, if due to the fact that the pot has been raised once or twice, you suspect that someone has a pair of Aces or Kings in the pocket, because of the increased potential of improving your hand, a hand that is much lower rated might be preferable to a hand that contains an unpaired Ace and/or King.

Categories of Starting Hands

Category 1 - Excellent Starting Hands

A - A   J - J
K - K   A - K (of same suit)
Q - Q

Category 2 - Good Starting Hands

10 - 10	9 - 9
A - Q (of same suit)	A - J (of same suit)
A - K	K - Q (of same suit)

Category 3 - Usually Playable Hands

Q - J (of same suit)	A - Q
J - 10 (of same suit)	10 - 9 (of same suit)
K - J (of same suit)	8 - 8
A - 10 (of same suit)	7 - 7

Category 4 - Sometimes Playable Hands

- Any pair smaller than 7s.
- Any cards of same suit that are consecutive in rank but smaller than 10-9.
- Any connected but not suited cards in which the smaller of the cards is at least a 5.
- Any two cards ranked higher than a 10 that are not of the same suit.

Category 1 hands consist of big pairs and a two-card combination that has the potential to make a big pair as well as a big flush or straight. With one of these hands, the object should be to build the pot and make players with lesser hands pay to play against you. It is therefore usually wise to raise with one of these hands. However, if you are playing no-limit Texas Hold'em, you would normally not want to raise such a large amount that all the other players would fold their hands, unless there is already a substantial amount of money in the pot.

Category 2 hands consist of two fairly large pairs and some two-card combinations that have excellent potential to make a winning hand. Depending on your position and your assessment of the situation, you can raise with one of these hands. However, unless you think that you might be able to isolate a player who has raised the pot recklessly ahead of you, I would not re-raise with one of these hands.

Category 3 hands are usually playable. However, if there is indication of substantial action before the flop, do not hesitate to abandon the hand.

Category 4 hands are normally playable only when possible to do so at nominal cost. Do not raise, especially from an early position, because that will tend to discourage callers. When playing one of these hands, what you usually want is a large number of players because that will give you the pot odds that you need. This is especially true when playing small pocket pairs.

The foregoing is not intended to imply that hands that are not indicated above should never be played. A truism of Texas Hold'em is that "any two cards can win." If possible to call at nominal cost, I would recommend that you sometimes call with mediocre cards such as 4 and 5 that are not even suited, especially if you are in one of the "blind" positions.

In casinos, Texas Hold'em is played with what are known as blinds. A blind is a player who is required to make a call before receiving his pocket cards. Normally, the player to the immediate left of the dealer, who is referred to as the "small blind," is required to deposit one half of the opening bet, and the next player, who is known as the "big blind," is required to deposit an amount equal to the full amount of the opening bet. For example, if the required opening bet is $2, the small blind is required to deposit $1 and the big blind is required to deposit $2. Therefore, if there has not been a raise, the player that was in the small blind position would only need to pay an additional $1 in order to play his hand, and the player who is in the big blind position would not be required to pay any additional amount to play his hand.

One of the most common mistakes that a novice will make when playing Texas Hold'em in a casino is the failure to properly consider the pot odds when in the small blind position and the pot has not been raised. If the big blind is $2 and four players have called when you are in the small blind position, it will cost you only an additional $1 to call. Since there will already be $11 in the pot, you will be getting odds of 11 to 1 to make the call.

This means that it might be wise to make the call even if you have what would otherwise be considered a mediocre starting hand. An important factor to be considered in such a situation is that the players who have called before you probably have big cards in the pocket. Therefore, if you have small cards in the pocket, you are probably holding cards that are more likely to appear on the flop than the other players.

A word of caution in evaluating starting hands. There is a tendency among inexperienced Texas Hold'em players to seriously overestimate the value of starting hands that contain two small cards that are of the same suit. With two cards of the same suit, the chance of making a flush with the five cards that will appear on the table is only 6.5%. The obvious message here is that two suited cards in the pocket are of little value unless they are both big cards or also have straight potential. Another problem with playing two small suited cards is the high potential for taking a bad beat, because another player will make a higher flush, either because he has two higher cards of the suit in the pocket or a fourth card of that suit appears on the table.

After the Flop

Because the first round of betting takes place when players have seen only two of their cards, there is not usually a great deal of betting and raising before the flop. It is therefore generally possible to see the flop without making a large financial commitment to your hand. Since you will usually not have much of an investment in a hand until after the flop, it is extremely important to properly evaluate your prospects before deciding to proceed further.

After the flop, you will be looking at 60% of the eventual board (3 of the 5 cards), but will usually have little invested in the hand. If you started with a small pocket pair and the flop does not give you a set (three of a kind), be inclined to fold if there is any significant action. If you do flop the set, be aggressive. Do not let your rivals draw to potential straights and flushes too cheaply.

Some players do not seem to realize that when a pair appears on the board, it is probably more likely to harm a player who started with a small pocket pair than it is to help that player. For example, assume that you have a pair of 5s in the pocket and the board shows:

Although the pair of 4s on the board will have improved your hand to two pair, your two pair will lose to any player who has a 4, 8, J, or K in the pocket. This is the reason why if you started with a small pair in the pocket, you will almost always need to make a set in order to have a reasonable chance to win the pot.

Be prepared to abandon even a premium starting hand if the flop appears to be dangerous, but does not help you. For example, assume that you have:

And the flop is:

If there is significant action, don't hesitate to abandon the Aces because it would be prudent to assume that you will probably need to make a full house in order to win the pot. However, notice that if one of your Aces were the Ace of diamonds, you would have had a chance to make an Ace-high flush.

Beware of drawing hands that appear to have potential, but actually give you very little chance to win. As an example of one such situation, assume that your pocket cards are:

And the board shows:

Although you have an open-ended straight draw, if there is action after this flop, it is very possible that someone already has a straight. At a minimum, it would be prudent to assume that at least one player has a higher pair than your eights. Note, however, that if another eight appears on the board, it becomes highly probable that at least one of the other players will have a straight. This, therefore, is a hand that should be played with extreme caution.

Estimate the strength of an opponent's hand based on that player's action prior to the flop. For example, if a player has bet or raised aggressively before the flop, it is likely that his pocket cards are a big pair or two high cards with straight and/or flush potential. Therefore, if the board shows:

and he has made a bet, it is probably safe to assume that he has two pair. You should therefore consider a raise if you have an 8 in your hand, even if your other card (your "kicker") is small. However, if the player who had bet a board such as this had been passive before the flop, it is likely that he also has a set and that his kicker is larger than yours. There is also the possibility that a player who has bet this board is bluffing. In either case, a raise would probably not be wise.

Sizing Up The Competition

The vast majority of poker players who play regularly in a casino compete in the same game for the same stakes. In other words, although almost all of them will try other games from time to time, casino poker players tend to specialize in a game of their choice. Therefore, for the most part, they acquire a reasonable amount of skill in that game of choice. However, because of the house rake, tips, and the high overall caliber of play in the casinos, in the long run, it is extremely difficult to win money playing poker in casinos. In fact, in the smaller limit games, it is all but impossible to win in the long run. At best, the wise small stakes players look upon casino poker as a recreational outlet in which they might occasionally be able to pick up some additional spending money from tourists.

At the higher limits, because the house rake is lower relative to the size of the pots, it is possible to be a long-term winner. However, as the stakes increase, so does the skill level of the players. As a result, only a small number of highly-skilled players can hope to be successful in these high-stakes games. Notwithstanding the foregoing, it is not the intent of the author to discourage you from trying your hand at casino poker. If you enjoy playing poker and are the type of player who gives serious thought to the game, I encourage you to give it a try. I believe that you will find it to be an interesting and challenging experience. However, before you sit down at any poker table, be sure that you are comfortable with the stakes and don't be intimidated. You cannot possibly lose more money than you are willing to put on the table. In a sense, the casino poker room is like any other casino venue. You will not risk financial ruin as long as you remain in control of your senses, so relax and don't let anybody at the table push you around.

Any experienced casino poker player can spot a greenhorn as soon as he sits down at the table. However, an astute greenhorn can usually spot the regulars. A regular player will generally be intimately familiar with the house rules and will probably be relaxed and comfortable. He will also know many of the dealers, as well as some of the other players. Look for lighthearted banter between them about recent or upcoming sporting events.

It is important to be able to pick out the regulars because that will give you important clues about how they can be expected to play. Most regulars will play fairly conservatively because if they played otherwise, they would not survive long enough to qualify as a regular. If you see a player whom you assume to be a regular, call a raise before the flop when he was not in one of the blind positions, you should certainly assume that he has at least a decent starting hand. Likewise, you should assume that he understands the concept of pot odds, and will probably not let you steal a large pot with a small bet. You can also expect that he will understand enough about position poker to know when he might be able to bluff you out of a pot. However, do not fear that the competition at a small stakes table may be unbeatable. After all, if the player was that strong, why would he be playing at a small stakes table?

Jackpots and Rakes

Casinos make money in their poker room by raking pots. In other words, they take chips out of the pot before pushing the pot to the player who had the winning hand. The rake usually varies from 3% to 5% of the amount that was in the pot, but in some smaller limit games, the rake might run higher. Many casino players fail to appreciate the full impact of the house rake. Because the rake is based on the total amount that was in the pot, the actual impact on winning is substantially greater. For example, if only one other player was in the hand and you win a $50 pot, your actual winnings will be approximately $25. If the house rake is 5%, the dealer will deduct $2.50, which amounts to 10% of the amount that you would otherwise have won. It gets even worse because most casinos round up to the nearest dollar. However, there is usually an upper limit on the amount that will be deducted from a pot. In some casinos, instead of raking a percentage of the pot, a fixed amount is deducted from each pot.

The rake is the primary reason why almost all casino poker players lose money in the poker room. In essence, the rake amounts to a rent that you are being charged for your seat at the table and should be treated as part of the cost of your entertainment. Before renting anything, it is wise to find out beforehand what it will cost. Don't be shy about asking one of the floor men before sitting down at a table. Many casinos have information sheets that spell out how pots are raked. However, you can easily determine the approximate amount of the rake by watching while a few hands are played.

In many casinos, you will notice that the house dealer will drop most of the chips that she rakes into a slot on the table, but will drop one chip into a different slot. The chip that is dropped into the second slot is for the "bad beat" jackpot pool that will be paid out when one of the players loses a pot in spite of having what is generally regarded to be a virtually unbeatable hand. In most cases, the player who lost the jackpot hand will receive 50% of the jackpot pool, the player who had the winning hand will receive 25% and all other players who participated in the jackpot hand will split the remaining 25%.

The minimum jackpot qualifying hand is usually a full house consisting of three Aces accompanied by a pair of 10s, Jacks, Queens, or Kings. This means that the losing hand must be at least a very potent full house. There are usually the following additional conditions:

- The jackpot qualifying hand must be beaten by at least four of a kind

• The player who is holding the winning hand and the player who is holding the losing hand must use both of their pocket cards to complete a jackpot-qualifying hand.

For example, assume that the following cards appear on the table:

A player who has an Ace and a King in the pocket will not have a jackpot-qualifying hand because although he will have a full house consisting of three Aces and two Jacks, he would not be using both of his pocket cards to complete his otherwise jackpot-qualifying hand. However, if he had an Ace and a Queen, he would have a jackpot-qualifying hand consisting of three Aces and a pair of Queens. All he would then need in order to hit the jackpot is another player at the table who has a pair of Jacks in the pocket!

Because it is extremely difficult to win a jackpot, jackpot pools have been known to increase to as much as $50,000 for even small stakes games. The result is some rather strange play. For example, assume that you have called with two deuces in the pocket and the other two deuces appear on the flop. You will then have a hand that is virtually certain to win the pot. However, if the hand loses, you might win a jackpot that could result in an astronomical profit. It would therefore be in your best interest to try to maximize your chances of losing. This means that it would not be wise to bet or raise until after the river card has been placed on the table because you would not want to do anything that might discourage another player from making a miracle draw to beat your four deuces.

Poker jackpot rules are complex and may vary considerably between casinos, even those that may be in close proximity.

Fortunately, most casinos make flyers available that explain their jackpot rules. Be sure that you read the flyer before sitting down at a jackpot table.

Many experienced poker players, the author included, do not look with favor on jackpot poker because it introduces a "crapshoot" element to what is supposed to be a game of skill. Another objection is that the additional drop for the jackpot pool unduly drains money from the table. Unfortunately, casino managers love jackpot poker because the potential of a big payout attracts patronage.

Poker Tells

A "tell" is an act or mannerism that may give an indication of the strength of a player's hand. Because we are all mortals, all poker players have tells. However, the tell may be as obvious as a rank amateur practically shouting "I raise" when he makes a strong hand or so innocuous as to be virtually undetectable. It goes without saying that the astute observer must also consider the possibility that a tell might be faked in an attempt to deceive other players at the table. "All's fair in love, war and poker."

Entire books have been written on the subject of poker tells. However, following are some of the most basic tells that you might encounter at a small stakes table in a casino.

Tell # 1: Closely Guarding Cards

If you notice that one of the players seems to be taking extra care to protect his pocket cards on a particular hand, proceed with caution. There is no need to take extra precautions to protect cards that will be discarded. Therefore, this is almost always an indication that the player in question has excellent cards in the pocket.

Tell #2: Preparing to Discard Hand

Inexperienced players frequently act on their hand and discard (or prepare to discard) their hand prematurely. Obviously, this can be very useful information, especially if you are considering a bluff. However, if that player then raises a bet, proceed with caution.

Tell #3: Showing Cards to a Neighbor

A player who has a strong hand is usually reluctant to show his pocket cards to others until it is time to do so. If a player is showing a neighbor his hand prematurely, it almost always indicates that the player missed making a strong hand and is soliciting sympathy.

Tell #4: Double Checking Pocket Cards

If a player checks his pocket cards after a new card appears on the table, that usually indicates that a player is checking to see if the new card gave him potential. For example, if the flop contained two hearts and the turn card was also a heart, a player who checks his pocket cards is probably checking to see if he has a heart in the pocket because he would then have a chance to make a flush. If he had two hearts in the pocket, he probably would have known that the third heart on the board gave him a flush and there would have been no need to check after the turn card had been exposed.

Tell #5: Betting With a Shrug

A player who bets with a shrug is trying to convey an air of indifference. It would therefore be prudent to assume that he has at least a reasonably strong hand. However, a player who calls a bet with a shrug is usually not trying to fool anyone and probably has a hand that is only considered to have a reasonably good chance to win the pot. Therefore, if you have a hand that is good enough to raise the original bettor, the player who called with a shrug should not deter you from raising.

Tell #6: Looking Bored

A player who looks bored while continuing to play a hand will frequently have a strong hand or a hand with excellent potential. After all, if the cards that he is holding are so boring, why doesn't he simply discard them and go for a walk? Be especially wary of a player who appears to be more bored than usual.

Tell #7: Momentarily Glancing at Chips

If a player glances at his stack of chips and then bets unhesitatingly when a new card appears on the table, this is usually an indication of strength. The glance will normally be fleeting and, therefore, difficult to detect unless you are watching closely.

In a similar but entirely different tell, if a player appears to be counting his stack of chips (rather than just momentarily glancing at the stack), then calls a bet, it is usually safe to assume that the player was unconsciously trying to decide if he can afford to make the call. Therefore, this player probably has a decent, but not necessarily strong, hand.

Tell #8: The Hesitation Bet

If a player who was preparing to bet suddenly stops to check his pocket cards when he sees another player reaching for chips in order to call the bet, the first player probably has a marginal hand that may not have justified a bet. The reason is that if he had a truly strong hand, he would have known exactly what he had before he decided to bet the hand.

In a related fake tell, some players who have a potential calling hand will reach for chips prematurely in an attempt to discourage a player from making a bet.

Tell #9: Uninvolved Player Tells

Some of the most reliably and useful tells are the tells that are exhibited by players who have already folded their hand. For example, if the flop includes two Jacks and you notice that a player who has discarded his hand squirms when the house dealer turned over the flop cards, you can probably safely assume that he folded with a Jack in the pocket. This can be very useful information because it greatly reduces the possibility that one of the other players made a set on the flop. Obviously, if you have a Jack in the pocket, that would put you in an extremely strong position.

Poker Tournaments

No discourse on casino poker would be complete without mention of poker tournaments.

With the introduction of the *World Poker Tour* on television a few years ago, poker tournaments have become extremely popular in casinos. However, poker tournaments that are being televised are mostly high-stakes no-limit tournaments with entry fees of as much as $50,000. Obviously, such tournaments are not for the average recreational poker player. However, many of the large casinos also conduct small-stakes tournaments with entry fees that are as low as $25. Most of these tournaments allow re-buys for the first hour of play and are conducted during the middle of the day when business is slow. Because such tournaments are not intended to be moneymakers, but are intended to attract customers into the casino, there is no house rake. Instead, a small service charge (usually $5 to $10 for each player) is included in the entry fee. Except for this service fee, all receipts are paid out to the players and the house usually guarantees a minimum amount for the tournament prize pool. Typically, this guarantee is $1,500 to $2,000.

Because the amount of the service charge is usually quite small relative to the size of the tournament prize pool, these small stakes poker tournaments are among the best bargains in the casino. However, for the casual drop-in player, there are two drawbacks.

- You must be in the casino at the start of the tournament in order to sign up.

- If you hope to share in the tournament pool, you must be prepared to play for the two to four hour duration of the tournament.

Tournaments are conducted for most of the more popular games that are being played in the casino poker room. However, by far the most popular tournament game is no-limit Texas Hold'em. The reason is that no-limit tournaments tend to end quickly and casino management wants to free up tournament players for the regular tables where the casino will be able to rake each pot.

In any poker game, a key element to success is knowledge of how other players are playing. In the early stages of a tournament, how players acquired their chips is the key determining factor. In a poker tournament, players will acquire chips in the following ways.

For "no re-buy tournaments," players generally receive a large amount of chips relative to the opening blinds. For example, players might be given as much as $500 in tournament chips with opening blinds of only $5 and $10. However, the blinds will increase very rapidly, usually at 15 or 20-minute intervals.

Because it seems cheap, many players have a tendency to play very recklessly during the early stage of these tournaments. Do not fall into this trap. Later on, one chip can mean the difference between qualifying for a share of the tournament pool or leaving empty handed. Play solid, sensible poker. However, if you think that you have the best hand or the hand with the most potential, be aggressive and take advantage of the loose play of others.

The initial stack for a "one re-buy tournament" is usually smaller than the no re-buy tournament. However, since most of the players will plan to make the re-buy, the action usually proceeds in much the same manner as a no re-buy tournament. In general, after a player has lost his initial stack of chips and made his one authorized re-buy, you can expect him to play more conservatively.

The majority of small stakes poker tournaments are "multiple re-buy tournaments." In these tournaments, players are allowed to make an unlimited number of re-buys until the intermission, which usually comes after one hour of play. However, a player must have less than a specified number of chips in order to qualify to make a re-buy.

There are two types of re-buy tournaments. In a "constant stack re-buy tournament," the number of chips that a player receives for a re-buy remains constant throughout the re-buy period. Because they can readily replenish their stack, many players play far too loosely in the early stages of these tournaments. What these players fail to properly consider is that when they qualify to make a re-buy, they have done so by putting additional chips in the hands of rivals. In view of the loose play of others, it would definitely be wise to relax your own calling and betting standards. Also, tend to be aggressive when you think that you are in the lead.

In a "progressive stack re-buy tournament," the number of chips that a player receives increases as the tournament progresses. In a typical tournament of this type, the initial stack might consist of $200 in tournament chips. If a re-buy is made during the first twenty minutes, the player receives an additional $200 in tournament chips. After twenty minutes, the betting limit increases and the re-buy stack increases to $300. After another twenty minutes, the betting limits again increase and the re-buy stack increases to $400. There are no further increases in the re-buy stack.

In a tournament of this type, action usually starts slowly because nobody wants to be forced to buy chips at $200 for a fixed amount of money when he knows that he will later be able to get $400 for that same amount of money in a few more minutes. However, action will pick up as the re-buy stack increases. In a tournament of this type, because you will be getting excellent value for your money, you should make all the re-buys that you can after the re-buy stack has increased to the maximum. Also, if possible, you should strive to force other players to make re-buys before the re-buy stack increases to the maximum level. In other words, if you are in a hand with a fairly large stack against another player who has a small stack when the re-buy stack is only $200, be inclined to put the pressure on him and bet or raise in a situation in which you might otherwise have merely checked or called.

The middle stage of a tournament begins after the first intermission, which usually comes after one hour of play. Because re-buys are no longer permitted, players will have a tendency to become more conservative. Tournament poker is a contest of survival with the last few players sharing in the tournament pool. However, because the blinds and betting limits will increase rapidly, it is not possible to survive by sitting on your stack. At this stage of a tournament, you should play conservatively, but aggressively. By that, I mean that you should select your starting hands wisely, but when you decide to play a hand, be aggressive.

In the final stages of a tournament, you will find that most of the players who have short stacks are playing very conservatively because they are just trying to survive long enough to share in the tournament pool. This is the time to take advantage of the tight play of others to steal the blinds, especially if you are in a late position with a large stack and the players in the blind positions have small stacks.

Following is an example of how a typical $2,000 tournament pool might be shared. However, depending on the number of players who had entered the tournament, a small amount might be paid to additional players.

Distribution of a Poker Tournament Pool

Place	Amount Paid	Percentage
1st	$800	40%
2nd	440	22
3rd	280	14
4th	160	8
5th	120	6
6th	80	4
7th	50	2.5
8th	40	2.0
9th	30	1.5
Totals:	**$2,000**	**100.0%**

Because the blinds and betting limits are very high in the last stages of a poker tournament and there is a relatively large difference between amounts that will be paid to the last few players, the turn of one card can mean the difference of hundreds of dollars. There is, therefore, an incentive for the last few players to negotiate a settlement and few of these small-stakes tournaments are actually played to conclusion.

If you find yourself in a position to negotiate a settlement, always bear in mind that the amount of money that is being negotiated is not the amount of money that is left in the tournament pool, but the amount that has not already been guaranteed to each of the remaining players. For example, if the last three players are discussing settlement of the tournament pool that has been illustrated above, the actual amount that is being negotiated is not $1520 ($800+$440+$280), but $680 ($1520 minus three times $280). Each player is assured of at minimum, a third place finish with a $280 payout, so no one will settle for less than that amount. It is the additional money for the second and first place finishes that needs to be allocated. As a result, the actual value of a small stack will usually be considerably greater than might be assumed from a casual comparison of the stacks of the three remaining players. Obviously, in games such as Texas Hold'em, the position of the dealer button can be extremely important because if you are in the dealer position, on the next hand that is played, you will not be required to commit any of your chips until after you have seen your pocket cards.

Numerous books have been published on the subject of poker tournaments. However, most of these books are directed towards players who are already familiar with poker tournaments. An exception is my *Poker Tournament Strategies,* which was first published in 1998, quite some time before poker tournaments became a staple on TV. *Poker Tournament Strategies* is a basic primer on poker tournaments and was intended for those who have had little or no previous poker tournament experience. If you are interested in acquiring additional information on poker tournaments and how the various types of tournaments should be played, you will find this book of interest.

Part V

Epilogue

Good Bets and Bad Bets

Glossary

16. Good Bets and Bad Bets

In previous chapters, the most popular games and gaming venues that can be found in the typical American casino were discussed at varying lengths. Following are brief summaries of some of the more popular good bets and bad bets that were mentioned. Within the good bet and bad bet categories, bets are listed in the order in which they appear in the book.

Good Bets

• **Banker Hand Bet (Chapter 2).** A bet on the banker hand to win at a baccarat (or mini-baccarat) table gives the casino a modest 1.2% house advantage over the bettor, making this one of the best bets that are available in a casino. A bet on the player hand gives the casino a slightly higher 1.4% house advantage, also a relatively good bet. The only other bet that can be made at a baccarat table is a bet that the two hands will tie. However, because the casino will enjoy an unreasonably high 14% advantage, this is a bet that should be avoided.

• **Blackjack (Chapter 3).** For many years, it was assumed that because the dealer acted on her hand after the player, and the player would frequently bust out before the dealer acted, the dealer had a huge advantage at a blackjack table. However, a series of computer studies conducted by respected mathematicians and scientists over the last 50 years indicates that with optimal play, it is possible to reduce the dealer advantage to less than 1%. Therefore, if played optimally with proper basic strategy, the blackjack table offers many of the best bets in the casino.

However, basic strategy, which is discussed in Chapter 3, is complex and requires fine tuning in order to compensate for the fact that there are some differences in the way that blackjack is played in the various casinos. It has also been proven that the ability to count cards can help players take advantage of favorable situations that will result when the unused portion of the deck contains an inordinately high number of Aces and ten-valued cards.

• **Pass Line Bet Combined With an Odds Bet (Chapter 4).** When a shooter at the craps table makes his first roll of the dice (the come-out roll), the casino has a 1.41% house advantage over the shooter in spite of the fact that the shooter is more likely to roll a 7 or 11 (a natural), which is an automatic winner, than a 2, 3 or 12 (a craps), which is an automatic loser. However, if the come-out roll produces a "point" (4, 5, 6, 8, 9 or 10), which will be the case in 2 out of 3 instances, the shooter becomes as much as a 2 to 1 underdog. Because the casino allows the shooter (including patrons who have bet with the shooter) an opportunity to take odds on the point at true odds, bettors can reduce the initial 1.41% house advantage by taking odds on the point at true odds. Since the casino does not enjoy a house advantage on the odds bet, the odds bet is usually limited to two times the amount of the original pass line bet. The net effect of taking odds on the total amount that was wagered is as follows.

Effect of the Odds Bet in Craps

Amount of the Odds Bet	House Advantage
No odds bet made	1.41%
Equal to pass line bet	.85%
Double amount of pass line bet	.61%

A come bet followed by an odds bet and a don't pass bet followed by a laying (giving) odds bet will produce similar odds. However, because the action at a craps table is usually hectic and can become very confusing, unless you are an experienced craps player, it is recommended that you initially limit yourself to making a pass line bet and then take odds on the point.

• **Video Poker with Progressive Jackpots (Chapter 12).** Computer studies indicate that a video poker machine with an 8-5 Jacks or Better payout table becomes a positive expectation instrument when the payout for a royal flush reaches 8,800 credits. However, in order to qualify for this large payout, the machine must be played for maximum credits. This means that on a $1 machine, $5 must be committed on each play. Unfortunately, progressive jackpot machines, with an 8-5 payout table, are now difficult to find. Another problem is that when a positive expectation develops, "regulars" who are on the lookout for such opportunities tend to monopolize the machine. Obviously, when giving consideration to playing such a machine, it would be wise to consider the fact that playing five credits on each "spin" might result in putting at risk more money than might be wise.

• **Small Stakes Poker Tournaments (Chapter 15).** During late morning or early afternoon hours when business is slow, many casinos that have poker rooms conduct small stakes poker tournaments. Because these tournaments are not intended to be moneymakers, but are intended to attract customers into the casinos, entry fees tend to be very modest. In fact, a guaranteed prize pool frequently exceeds the amount that the casino will collect from entry fees. If you are an even moderately accomplished small stakes player, you will probably find these tournaments to be enjoyable, as well as possibly profitable. First, however, I would suggest that you carefully read Chapter 15 because in poker tournament play, there are nuances that you will not encounter at a regular poker table.

Bad Bets

• **Big 6 and Big 8 Bets at a Craps Table (Chapter 4).**The Big 6 and Big 8 bets are even money bets that the 6 or 8 will appear before the 7. Since there are six combinations of the dice that will total 7, but only five combinations that will total 6 and 8, the casino will enjoy a 9.1% advantage on these two bets.

Although there are many bets in a casino that will give the house an even bigger house advantage, the Big 6 and Big 8 bets deserve to be mentioned in this Bad Bets section because a craps player can also make a place bet on the 6 or 8 that will pay $7 on a $6 bet. Why risk $5 to win $5 when the same bet can be made that will return $7 on a $6 bet?

• **Keno (Chapter 10).** With the poorest overall odds and payoffs in the casino, keno is not the game for anyone who is serious about winning money in a casino. However, it does have the advantage of being very low key and providing an opportunity for someone who is relaxing in the pool area or cocktail lounge to participate in the gaming. Keno also has the advantage of accepting small bets and offering an opportunity to pursue potentially huge payouts.

• **Slot Machines with Large Progressive Jackpots (Chapter 11).** According to the California State Lottery Commission, the odds against hitting the six-number state lottery are 41,416,353 to 1, and the largest jackpot pool ever was $193 million. At $193 million, a ticket for the state lottery had a very substantial positive expectation. Does this mean that a $1 investment in a lottery ticket was a good investment? Yes and no. Yes, because it had a positive expectation, but no because the odds against hitting the jackpot are always 41,416,353 to 1.

In many respects, a slot machine with a progressive jackpot can be far more detrimental to a gambler's pocketbook than a state lottery. It is relatively easy to find out what the odds are in a state lottery. On slot machines, such information is a closely guarded secret, but in some cases, can be as astronomical as a state lottery. In a state lottery, the cost is nominal and is usually readily controllable. On a slot machine, the cost can be very high. For example, in order to qualify for the progressive jackpot on even a penny machine, the cost for one "spin" is more than $2, and many patrons find it difficult to resist the urge to "chase." Incidentally, figures released by the Nevada Gaming Control Board indicate that for 2006, the "win" for all $1 slot machines in Nevada was $1.0 billion. For penny machines, the win was $1.3 billion. The win is defined as the total amount that was wagered on the machines, minus the amount that was paid out.

The reader probably will have noticed that unlike a slot machine with a progressive jackpot, a video poker machine with a progressive jackpot was listed among the good bets in the casino. The differences are that (1) it is relatively easy to determine when a video poker machine has become a positive expectation instrument and (2) with optimal play, the odds of hitting the jackpot are "only" about 40,000 to 1.

• **Blackjack and Keno on Video Machines (Chapter 12).** The problem with blackjack on a video machine is that most machines pay only even money (rather than 3 to 2) on a blackjack, and do not allow the splitting of pairs or double-down when the first two cards total 10 or 11. Without these and other important player advantage features, the house advantage is simply too great. The problem with keno on these machines is that the machines generally have the same long odds and poor payouts as the keno lounge. The one favorable feature of video keno is that the smaller denomination machines offer the opportunity to pursue a relatively large payout for as little as a nickel per spin.

• **Sports Parlay Bets (Chapter 13).** On the typical sports bet that is made in a casino, the house enjoys an advantage of 5-6%. However, on a parlay, the casino enjoys a house advantage that frequently exceeds 35%. Avoid parlays, especially parlays of more than three games.

Glossary

Aces-up　　　A poker hand that contains a pair of Aces as well as a smaller pair.

across the board　　　Three bets at a racetrack that consist of one win bet, one place bet and one show bet that were purchased as a package.

action　　　The amount of money that was wagered.

all-in　　　In poker, a player who has already committed all of his chips and therefore cannot be raised.

allowance　　　A reduction in the amount of weight that a horse will be required to carry due to such factors as age, gender, experience at the distance to be run, etc.

ante　　　In some poker games, a nominal amount that must be wagered before cards are received.

bad beat	A poker term that is applicable when a player loses a pot in spite of the fact that he had a very strong hand or was at one time a heavy favorite to win the pot.
banker	The entity that pays winning bets and receives losing bets. In most cases, the casino itself serves as the banker. However, in some cases, one of the players might be serving as the banker.
basic strategy	A program of optimal choices that will maximize the chance of winning.
Big Dick	In craps, slang for ten.
blind bet	In some poker games, a bet that one or two of the players are required to make before receiving cards.
bluff	In a poker game, to bet or raise with a weak hand in the hope that other players will be deceived into discarding a stronger hand.
board	The five common cards that are dealt-face up on the poker table in Texas Hold'em and Omaha games.
bones	Slang for dice.
book	An organization that establishes odds and/or accepts bets on sporting events. Also a bookie or bookmaker.

Box Cars	In craps, a roll in which a six appears on each of the two die.
brick	At a poker table, a useless card.
bring-in	In Seven-Card Stud poker, a nominal bet that the player with the lowest card showing on the first round of betting is required to make.
buck	Casino slang for $100.
burn card	The top card on a deck of cards that is discarded by the dealer before continuing to deal.
bust	To go over 21 at a blackjack table.
bust out	To run out of money.
button	A device that is used to indicate which player is serving as the player dealer.
buy-in	The minimum amount of money that is needed in order to enter a game.
call	In poker, the act of matching a bet that was made by another player. In bingo and keno, the act of drawing a number that will appear on the board.
carousel	A cluster of gaming machines that have been arranged in a circle or ring for ease of management.

casino rate	A reduced rate, usually for rooms, that a casino offers in order to reward previous patrons or attract new patrons.
catch	In keno, a "catch" occurs when a number that was marked on a keno ticket lights up on the keno board.
chase	To gamble recklessly in the hope of recouping previous losses.
check	Synonymous with casino chip. In poker, to decline to bet.
chip	An instrument that is used in lieu of cash.
cold	When gambling, a synonym for unlucky.
come out roll	At a craps table, the first roll of the dice for a player who has not yet established a point.
community card	In poker, a card that serves as part of every player's hand.
comp	A gift or service that is given without charge in a casino. Most, but not all comps, were earned by previous patronage.
copy	(1) In pai gow poker, a copy occurs when one of the player's hands is identical to that of the banker. The

banker wins all copies. (2) In regular American style poker, a copy is said to occur when one of the cards on the board pairs a card that a player already had, but the pair does not result in creating a winning hand.

croupier
The French word for dealer. Commonly used at baccarat and roulette tables.

dead heat
Racetrack terminology for a race that ends in a tie.

dead money
Money that is brought to a poker table by a player who plays so poorly that he is thought to have little or no chance to win.

die
A cube that has one to six spots on each of the six sides. Singular for dice.

designated dealer
The player who is serving as the dealer for the current hand. Synonymous with player dealer.

do
Slang for a pass line bet or a come bet at a craps table.

dog
Synonymous with underdog. In poker, a bad card or a bad hand.

don't
Slang for a don't pass bet or a don't come bet at a craps table.

double-down   At a blackjack table, to double
                         the basic bet and accept only one
                         additional card.

drop box   A repository under a gaming table for
                         cash and chips.

early position   In poker, a position at a table that
                         will require the occupant to act on
                         his hand before most of the other
                         players at the table.

even money bet   A bet that will pay an amount that is
                         equal to the amount that was bet.

exacta   A bet in which the first two horses in
                         a race must be predicted in the exact
                         order in which they finish the race.
                         Also referred to as a perfecta.

face cards   All Jacks, Queens and Kings in a
                         deck of cards.

family pot   A pot in a poker game for which
                         many players are competing.

field   All participants in a game or event.

field bet   At a craps table, a bet that the next
                         number that is rolled will not be a 5,
                         6, 7 or 8.

filly   A female horse that is less than five
                         years old and has not been bred.

first base	In blackjack, the player who is seated to the dealer's immediate left and will therefore have the first option to draw additional cards or stand pat.
flat top	A gaming machine with a top prize that does not increase with additional play. See progressive machine.
flop	The first three cards that are turned face up on the table by the dealer in Texas Hold'em and Omaha games.
fold	The act of discarding a poker hand, thereby relinquishing any further claim to the pot.
fouled hand	A pai gow poker hand in which the two-card hand is stronger than the five-card hand. A fouled hand is an automatic loser.
furlong	One-eighth of a mile.
future bet	A bet that is made far in advance of the date that a winner can be determined.
give odds	To bet a favorite with the understanding that the amount that will be put at risk will be greater than the amount that can be won. Synonymous with lay odds.
gelding	A male horse that has been castrated.

handicapper

A person who analyzes data and predicts the outcome of sporting events.

handle

The total amount of money in a pari-mutuel pool.

hard hand

A blackjack hand that totals 12 or more and does not include an Ace that is being counted as 11. The hand can therefore bust (go over 21) with one additional card.

hardway

In craps, a 4, 6, 8 or 10 that is made by pairing the dice.

heads-up

In poker, a situation in which only two players remain in the hand.

hedge bet

A second bet that is the opposite of an earlier bet. Hedge bets are made in order to insure at least a nominal win or minimize a possible loss.

high roller

A patron who consistently bets a large amount.

hit

To take an additional card in blackjack.

Hold'em

Any of a variety of poker games in which five common cards that will become a part of each player's hand are turned face up on the table.

hole card

A card that is kept face down on the table until play has been completed.

house	Synonymous with casino. At the poker table, slang for a full house.
house advantage	The difference between the true odds and the amount that the casino will pay to winning bettors.
insurance	In blackjack, a side bet that the dealer has 21 with his first two cards. This bet is offered by the casino when the dealer's exposed card is an Ace.
jackpot	(1) The largest possible payout on a gaming machine. (2) In the poker room, a large special payout to a player who loses a pot in spite of having had an exceptionally strong hand. (3) In other venues, any large special payout.
juice	Synonymous with commission or vigorish.
lay odds	Synonymous with give odds.
line	A handicapper's point spread or odds which is intended to balance the betting between the competitors.
Little Joe	At the craps table, slang for four.
load up	To play a gaming machine for the maximum amount on each play (spin).
lock	A certainty.

loose	A gaming machine that has been paying out liberally. A poker player who plays too many hands.
maiden	At the racetrack, a horse or jockey that has never won a race.
maiden race	A race for horses that have never won a race.
mare	A female horse that is at least five years old. Also, a female less than five years old that has been bred.
marker	A check drawn against a credit account that a player has established in a casino.
money line	A betting line that is expressed in dollar amounts. If a favorite is bet, the amount that is put at risk will exceed the amount that can be won. If an underdog is bet, the amount that can be won will be greater than the amount that is put at risk.
monster	A very strong poker hand.
morning line	The opening odds at a race track.
muck	To discard playing cards. Also, the cards that were discarded.
mudder	A horse that runs well on a wet track.

natural	(1) In blackjack, any hand in which the first two cards total 21. (2) In baccarat, any hand in which the first two cards total 8 or 9. (3) In craps, a come out roll in which the dice total 7 or 11.
negative expectation	A game, situation or strategy which in the long run, can be expected to produce unfavorable results because of mathematical probability.
neutral site	A site at which neither of the competing teams will have a home field advantage.
nickel	Casino slang for $5.
nose	The smallest margin by which a horse can win a race.
nuts	A poker hand that cannot be beaten.
odds	Mathematical probability expressed as a ratio.
off the board	A game or sporting event for which no bets are being taken.
on a roll	To be on a hot streak.
one-roll bet	A wager at a craps table that will be determined on the next roll of the dice.

open
To commence the betting in a poker game.

opener
The player who made the first bet in a poker game.

over bet
A bet that the total number of points that will be scored during a game will be more than a specified amount.

over/under bet
A bet on the total number of points that will be scored during a game.

pari-mutuel pool
A wagering pool in which odds are established based on amounts that have been bet on each of the competitors.

parlay
To bet all of the money that was received from one bet on a subsequent bet.

parlay bet
A bet that is based on two or more games. Normally, in order to win a parlay bet, all teams that were selected must win.

pass
A winning roll for the shooter at a craps table.

pay line
A row of small windows on a slot machine under which certain symbols must appear in order to qualify for a payout. A machine may have more than one pay line.

payout	The amount that will be returned on a winning bet.
payout table	A schedule that indicates winning combinations and the amount that will be paid. For slot machines, the table is usually shown on the machine. On video gaming machines, tables will usually appear on the screen.
pit	An area around which a group of gaming tables are arranged.
point	At a craps tables, the number that the shooter is trying to repeat before a seven appears.
point spread	The number of points by which a favored team needs to win in order to reward its backers.
positive expectation	A game, situation or strategy which in the long run, can be expected to produce favorable results because of mathematical probability.
pot	The total amount of money that is at stake during play of a hand of poker.
probability	The likelihood that an event will occur.
progressive jackpot	A jackpot that increases with additional play until the jackpot is won. Then the jackpot will return to a predetermined starting point.

purse　　　　　　The total amount of money that will be distributed to winners of a race.

push　　　　　　Synonymous with tie.

quads　　　　　　In poker, slang for four of a kind.

qualifier　　　　　In a poker game in which the highest hand and the lowest hand will normally split the pot, the weakest low hand that will be eligible to share in the pot.

quarter　　　　　Casino slang for $25.

rack　　　　　　A tray for carrying coins, chips or tokens.

rags　　　　　　Cards that are of no value to a poker player.

raise　　　　　　At a poker table, to match a previous bet and bet an additional amount.

rake　　　　　　The amount of money that the casino deducts from the pot in a poker game as a service fee.

random number generator (RNG)　　　A computer chip in a gaming machine that will determine what symbols or cards will appear in the window of the machine.

reel　　　　　　A wheel in a slot machine that will display symbols that will appear in the window of the machine.

RFB	Abbreviation for room, food and beverages.
right bettor	A craps player who is betting that the player who is rolling the dice will succeed.
river	The last card that is dealt in Seven-Card Stud and Hold'em games.
rock	An extremely conservative poker player.
roll	One throw of the dice at a craps table.
scared money	Money that a player cannot afford to lose.
scoop	To win the entire pot in a poker game in which the player with the highest hand and the player with the lowest hand would normally split the pot.
scratch	To withdraw a horse from a race before the start of the race.
set	At a poker table, synonymous with three of a kind.
seven-out	To roll a seven, thereby losing the bet when trying to repeat a number (point) at a craps table.
shoe	A box or container from which cards are dealt to players.

side pot
A secondary pot that is created at a poker table when a player is unable to participate in further betting because he has no more chips on the table.

shooter
The player at a craps table who will throw (roll) the dice.

show
To finish third in a horse race.

show bet
A bet that a horse will finish first, second or third in a race.

showdown
The act of revealing cards after the completion of betting in poker.

Snake Eyes
At the craps table, a roll in which a one appears on each of the dice.

soft hand
A blackjack hand that includes an Ace but does not exceed 21 even if the Ace is counted as an 11. A soft hand therefore cannot bust (go over 21) with one additional card.

split
To separate a blackjack hand that includes two cards of equal value into two different hands.

stand
In blackjack, to decline to take an additional card.

stiff
A blackjack hand that would normally justify taking an additional card, but could go over 21 with that additional card.

sucker bet	A bet that gives the bettor very unfavorable odds.
surrender	To give up one half of the amount that was bet at a blackjack table rather than play out the hand.
table limit	The minimum and maximum amounts that may be wagered at a gaming table.
take odds	To bet an underdog with the prospect of winning a greater amount than was put at risk.
teaser	A multiple game sports parley bet that allows the bettor points that may be used to adjust established point spreads. However, the payout is much lower than for a regular parlay bet.
tell	An act or mannerism that may give an indication of the strength of a poker player's hand.
third base	In blackjack, the seat to the immediate right of the dealer.
tight	A gaming machine that is paying out poorly. At the poker table, a player who plays very conservatively.
toke	The casino term for tip.

tote board   A board that is used to display all current bets and odds at a racetrack.

tout   A person or firm that sells opinions on sporting events.

true odds   The mathematical probability that an event will occur.

trips   At the poker table, synonymous with three of a kind.

turn   At a poker table, the fourth community card.

under bet   A bet that the total number of points that will be scored in a game will be below a specified total.

up card   At a blackjack table, the dealer's card that is turned face up before players act on their hands. At a poker table, any card that is dealt face-up in a stud game

vigorish   A commission or fee that is charged by the casino.

way ticket   A keno ticket that provides for combining a given quantity of numbers in various ways in order to create multiple bets.

whale   A big bettor.

wrong bettor　　　　　A craps player who is betting that the shooter will not succeed.

Index

Coming in 2012......

Seven-Card Stud High-Low
(Eight or Better) Poker

Sam Braids

Get the edge in the least understood poker game

Seven-Card Stud High-Low Eight or Better is fundamentally different from Seven-Card Stud played for high hand only, but many players fail to understand the differences and make adjustments. In fact, it is one of the most complex, intricate and least understood variations of poker. For those reasons it is a profitable game to master. Players with knowledge of the game's subtleties and nuances will have a significant edge over your fellow players.

The definitive book on Stud High-Low

Mastering Stud High-Low is now essential to compete in mix-game events. The HORSE tournament format, which includes Stud High-Low, is now becoming the gold standard for poker expertise, and winning the HORSE tournament at the World Series of Poker is eclipsing the no-limit Hold'em Championship in prestige. Get the edge you need to be competitive with this detailed examination of the strategies, tactics, and mathematics of Stud High-Low. In it you will learn:

• Starting hand selection: It's very different than ordinary Seven-Card Stud
• The importance of the 4s and 5s: Next in importance to Aces, these are the cards to watch
• The dangers of 8s: found in many hands that trap the unprepared
• Essential concepts—scooping, free-rolling, nut low-hands
• Exclusive charts showing starting hand probabilities and odds for improvement
• Strategies and tactics for each stage of the hand

Be competitive in the hottest poker trend:
mixed-game events that include Stud High-Low!

Sam Braids, physicist and author of *The Intelligent Guide to Texas Hold'em Poker* (now in its second edition), has for decades studied and played poker and chess. He also holds a doctorate in physics, and has taught advanced physics and mathematics. A prolific writer on poker, he regularly contributes articles to *IntelligentPoker.com* and *StudHighLow.com*. He lives near Baltimore Maryland.

Look for in 2012 at http://www.StudHighLow.com

Expanded and Updated 2nd Edition to the International Bestseller
Texas Hold'em Poker
is (Still) the World's Most Popular Game

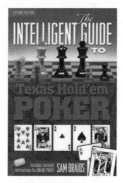

Whether you're an expert or a first-time player, this concise, comprehensive guide, is packed with tips and information you need to know. For beginners, you'll learn the rules of Texas Hold'em, basic strategy, and how to play in a cardroom. More advanced players will benefit from statistical charts, vignettes from actual poker games, and detailed information on how the social and psychological aspects of the game determine strategy.

Readers also learn the unique view that an expert chess player brings to analyzing poker, as author Sam Braids compares and contrasts the two games. Look inside for some of the charts and information—in highly usable formats—you can put to use right now:

• Expected profits for all 169 possible starting hands
• Probabilities for improving a hand
• 3-D charts showing the effect of position on profits
• Overcard probabilities
• Location and contact information for more than 200 cardrooms

Also Includes: An analysis of online poker, how to use your computer to play Internet poker, and explanations of the strategic adjustments necessary to succeed online.

"An excellent book for the losing player looking to win or for the novice looking to learn the game for the first time, Braids excels in explaining the sometimes-confusing concepts necessary for profitable Texas Hold'em play, by breaking down the subject into meaningful bite-sized pieces. He then includes many actual hand situations to illustrate the clear points he is making. This is a masterful book, and an excellent addition to the poker literature."

--Ashley Adams, Host of the radio show *House of Cards*

Order your copy at http://www.IntelligentPoker.com

ABOUT THE AUTHOR

Sylvester Suzuki, a 1959 graduate of the University of Washington, spent a 25-year career as a civilian administrative officer with several Department of Defense agencies, mostly overseas. Since his retirement in 1984 he has been a regular at the poker and gaming tables, primarily in the casinos of California and Nevada. He previously authored *Poker Tournament Strategies*. Currently he resides near Los Angeles.

ACKNOWLEDGEMENTS

The author, a "hunt and peck" typist who never had formal typing instruction and is also computer illiterate wishes to acknowledge the clerical, and especially technical assistance of Yuri Lily and Silvano Anastasi in preparing the manuscript for submission to the publisher. Their assistance was instrumental in getting this book into print. Many thanks. Grazie.